A GREAT WEEKEND IN

# DUBLIN

# A GREAT WEEKEND IN
# DUBLIN

Dublin is a capital unlike any other. Relatively small, it has managed to retain a rural feel, despite the concrete, with its tree-lined streets and spacious parks. The heart of the city, based around just a few streets, teems with literary and theatrical creativity, and is a magnet for poets and musicians. Dubliners revel in a convivial way of life and extend a warm welcome to visitors. The sky may be grey and the rain frequent, but at least you'll feel at home straight away.

The city is not as old as other European capitals, dating back just over a thousand years, and its constant evolution is clearly visible in the ever-present scaffolding and building repairs going on in and around the city. Its history blends British colonialism, poverty and revolutionary violence with a rich Celtic heritage. But little physical evidence remains of its troubled past. Many of Dublin's best-known monuments date back no further than the 18th century and the city's sober Georgian buildings are reminiscent of their architectural counterparts in cities across the water in England. Dublin's real wealth lies in the great figures of its past and in the people who live there today. You can find out more about the playwrights, poets and writers of the city – Joyce, Wilde, Yeats, Kavanagh, et al – by following one of the many literary tourist trails. But to locate the real pulse of the city, you'll need to spend time discovering some of the numerous dimly-lit pubs, listening to the rich variety of music on offer, engaging in conversations with the locals over a few

pints of Guinness and generally adapting to a different pace of life. Before long you'll find that the dusty streets and dismal weather are just a small part of this great city, which, little by little, completely captivates its visitors.

One of the immediate charms of Dublin is the constant sound of music. You'll find

buskers on every other street corner entertaining the passers-by, while in the pubs there's almost always someone singing or playing the flute, or penny whistle, the fiddle or the banjo. Ireland has produced a phenomenal amount of talented musicians over the years, many of whom have achieved worldwide fame and all of whom have contributed to the strong Irish tradition of music making. Whilst Dublin's new population supports one of the world's most vibrant rock scenes, the older, more traditional music continues to flourish alongside the new and the two styles, more often than not, influence each other. You'll be spoilt for choice with concerts and pub sessions throughout the capital and may well get the chance to hear some of the more well-known performers in action.

Dublin's shops are a must, too. They have always offered traditional, top-of-the-range products; the clothes rails feature hard-wearing tweeds, Aran jumpers, tartan kilts and hard-wearing oiled outdoor jackets, while in the homeware departments, the crystal and china are of the highest quality. With the recent economic boom, however, a whole new wave of modern and dynamic young designers have emerged on the scene, complementing the traditional ranges of clothes with more experimental and avant-garde designs. For many,

wearing traditional Irish tweed is still acceptable, as long as it's given a modern twist – a style that the new-generation designers have incorporated so well into their collections. In Grafton Street, the main city-centre shopping thoroughfare, these new designer boutiques are gradually replacing the former bastions of conservative ready-to-wear. In recent years, Dublin has also enjoyed success in IT and computer hardware development, becoming a cyberworld of new technology. The fiscal advantages enjoyed by the creative professionals have attracted newcomers with a more global outlook. This has resulted in an eclectic selection of new shops, restaurants and bars

springing up all over the city. On the whole, people are making the most of a new level of wealth previously unheard of. They enjoy spending their money and are proud of it – something new in a country where discretion has always been the rule. The regeneration of the Temple Bar district, with its lively bars, restaurants and artists' studios, is a perfect symbol of the city's rebirth.

Although you won't be able to see everything in a single weekend, you're sure to be tempted to come back again and again. On your first visit you can get a good feel for Dublin by just heading for Trinity College to see the illuminated manuscripts or by paying a quick visit to the National Museum. It's also worth wandering through the city squares, lined with tall Georgian houses, and along the green avenues and canals to give yourself a break from shopping. But, above all, you should head for a pub at the end of the day where you'll catch a real glimpse of Dublin life over a pint of Guinness or a warming shot of Irish whiskey.

# How to get there

There's no denying that it often rains in Ireland, but if you're dressed for the weather, it'll take more than a few showers to spoil your weekend in Dublin. Remember to pack a rain hat and you'll enjoy your stay.

## CLIMATE

Dublin has an oceanic climate, which means that it's temperate and wet. While rain is one of the hallmarks of Ireland, and Dublin has a fairly high proportion of rainy days annually, the actual amount of rainfall is quite low (750mm/29½in per year), because the rain is usually light and short-lived. The temperature varies little throughout the year (1-8°C/ 34-46°F in January, and 11-20°C/52-68°F in July), but the weather can change quickly. Wear plenty of layers, and always be prepared for rain. Remember, the wind is often strong, turning umbrellas inside out. If you mean to do a lot of walking, it's better to take a rain-hat.

Spring, from March to June, is the driest time of year, while the period from late August to December is the wettest. In winter, even when it doesn't rain, the air remains damp, making it feel colder. Pack at least one warm sweater and a raincoat, which will be more useful than an overcoat.

## WHEN TO GO

If you want to catch the sales, the best times to go are from just after Christmas to January, and in July. Mid-season sales take place halfway between these dates, in May and October. December is a very festive month, though not always in the best of taste, with Christmas carols played continuously over loudspeakers and garish decorations everywhere. Avoid Chrismas week proper as the city centre is empty and many restaurants and B&Bs close for the occasion. On the other hand, St Patrick's Day, the national holiday, which falls on 17 March (see p. 20), is a lively occasion. It's also the time of year when expats return to their families, all the hotels are full and prices rise steeply. The same can be said of Easter and the first weekends in May and June. The big sporting finals (Gaelic football, hurling and rugby) also bring noisy crowds to Dublin. Prices go through the ceiling and the drink flows freely. April, May, June and October are the quietest and most pleasant months.

# GETTING THERE

## FROM THE UK

### By Air

Flying is the most convenient way to reach Dublin. There are frequent flights to Dublin from London and regional airports and airlines such as Ryanair run promotional offers that make flying significantly less expensive than travelling by ferry.

### British Airways

☎ 0345 222 111
www.britishairways.com
BA runs up to 7 flights a day from Heathrow and 5 daily flights from Gatwick to Dublin, with connections to regional airports in the UK.

### Ryanair

☎ 0870 156 9569
www.ryanair.com
Ryanair flies to Dublin from Stansted, Gatwick and Luton up to 25 times in high season.

### Aer Lingus

☎ 0845 773 7747
www.flyaerlingus.com
Aer Lingus makes over 17 daily flights between London Heathrow, Gatwick, London City and Dublin.

### British Midland

☎ 0870 607 0555
www.iflybmi.com
British Midland flies up to eight times daily between London Heathrow and Dublin.

### By Coach

Eurolines runs four daily services from London Victoria Coach Station to Dublin, in partnership with Irish Ferries and Stena Line. Journey time is about 12 hours.

### Eurolines

☎ 0990 143219
www.eurolines.co.uk

### By Ferry

Several ferry companies sail routes from Britain to Ireland.

## USEFUL ADDRESSES

**Irish Tourist Offices Worldwide**

**UK:** 12 Regent Street
London SW1Y 4PQ
☎ 020 7839 8416

**USA:** Irish Tourist Board
345 Park Avenue
New York, NY 10154
☎ 212 418 0800

**Canada:** Suite 1150
160 Bloor Street East
Toronto M4W 1B9
☎ 416 929 2777

**Australia:** 36 Carrington
Street, Fifth Level
Sydney 2000
☎ 02 9299 6177

**In Ireland:** Baggot Street
Bridge, Dublin 2
☎ 01 602 4000

**Irish Embassies Abroad**

**UK:** 17 Grosvenor Place
London SW1Y 7HR
☎ 020 7235 2171

**USA:** 17th Floor
345 Park Ave
New York, NY 10154
☎ 212 433 7732

**Australia & New Zealand:**
20 Arkana Street
Yarralumla Act 260
Australia
☎ 02 6273 3022

Stena Line, in conjunction with Virgin Trains, offers a service from London to Dublin, Dun Laoghaire, crossing the Irish Sea at Holyhead, North Wales. Irish Ferries also sails from Holyhead to Dublin. The Sea Cat travels fast between Liverpool and Dublin.

**Stena Line**
☎ 0870 570 7070
www.stenaline.co.uk

**Irish Ferries**
www.irishferries.ie
☎ 0870 517 1717

**Sea Cat**
☎ 0870 552 3523

### FROM THE USA AND CANADA

Aer Lingus and Delta offer direct flights between the United States and Dublin. There are no direct flights between cities in Canada and Dublin. Canadian travellers should consider flying to London on airlines such as Air Canada or British Airways and then proceeding to Dublin by air or travelling via the United States.

**Aer Lingus**
☎ 212 557 1090
www.flyaerlingus.com
Daily flights from New York and flights three times a week from Los Angeles.

**Delta Airlines**
☎ 1 800 241 4141
www.delta.com
Daily flights from New York in summer, four flights weekly between October and April.

**British Airways**
☎ 1 800 AIRWAYS
www.britishairways.com
Regular direct flights from cities in the United States and Canada.

**Air Canada**
☎ 1 888 247 2262
www.aircanada.ca
Regular flights to Dublin from Toronto, Montreal, Vancouver and Ottawa.

### FROM AUSTRALIA AND NEW ZEALAND

Flights to Dublin from Sydney or Auckland usually involve at least two stops, once in Asia and finally in London to connect to Ireland.

**Qantas Airways**
☎ 02 231 5066
www.qantas.com

**Singapore Airlines**
☎ 02 844 0999
www.singaporeair.com

**Malaysia Airlines**
☎ 02 231 5066
www.malaysiaairlines.com

**Air New Zealand**
☎ 09 377 3886
www.airnz.co.uk

# FORMALITIES

Citizens of member states of the European Union only need a valid identity card or passport to enter Ireland. A minor travelling alone or with an adult who doesn't have custody rights will be required to produce parental permission to leave the country. Pets from countries other than the United Kingdom are subject to six months' quarantine. There are no exceptions.

## CUSTOMS

EU citizens no longer have to declare goods bought within the EU. Duty-free purchases are now reserved for non-EU citizens, the allowance per adult being 200 cigarettes (or 100 cigarillos or 50 cigars), 1l of spirits over 15°, 2l of wine and 50cl of perfume. Goods worth over IR£142/€180 must be declared.

## FROM AIRPORT TO CITY CENTRE

There are three ways of getting to the city centre: public transport, shuttle and taxi. Taxis are inevitably the most expensive option, but ideal if you arrive late.

### BY BUS

Several Dublin Bus Company lines run from the airport to the city centre: 33, 41, 41A, 41B and 41C. The journey takes around 45 minutes and costs IR£1.30/€1.65. The buses leave every 20-30 minutes and generally run 6am-11.30pm.

### BY SHUTTLE

More expensive (IR£3.50/€4.45) but faster than the bus, the **Airlink** shuttle (a yellow bus) leaves the airport every 10-20 minutes according to the time of day and serves the whole city centre. The **Aircoach** shuttle (a blue bus) leaves every 15 minutes to north and south city centres. It runs from 5am until 11.30pm and costs IR£4/€5.

### BY TAXI

You can get to the centre in 15-20 minutes, for IR£11-15/€14-19 depending on the number of passengers and items of luggage.

## BY CAR

If you're planning to bring your car over on the ferry, do check in advance with your hotel or place of accommodation that parking facilities are available. If possible, avoid taking your car into the city centre as traffic is dense and disorderly,

parking is costly and places are very limited. Car theft is also a problem.

### CAR HIRE

If you decide to hire a car, remember to take your driving licence. Most car hire companies only hire cars to drivers aged 23-70 years who have held a valid licence for at least two years. The speed limit is 50km/h (30mph) in built-up areas, 95km/h (60mph) outside built-up areas and 110km/h (70mph) on motorways. Seat belts must be worn in both the front and back seats. Parking offences are always punished and cars are often towed away. The price of petrol is around IR£0.73/€0.93 per litre, but can vary considerably from one petrol station to another. Car hire rates for a small car range from IR£23-37/€29-47 (including insurance) a day, depending on season. All the major car hire companies are represented at Dublin Airport.

**Avis**
☎ (01) 605 7500
**Hertz**
☎ (01) 844 5466
**Budget**
☎ (01) 844 5150
**National Car Rental**
☎ (01) 844 4162

## CURRENCY

At the time of writing, the currency is the Irish pound or *punt* (IR£), divided into 100 pence. Notes range from IR£100 to IR£5 and coins from IR£1 to 1p. On 9 February 2002, however, the pound ceases to be legal tender and Ireland's currency will be the euro (although you will still be able to change your notes in banks after this date). The euro, which is divided into 100 cents, has a fixed conversion rate of IR£0.787564. You can change your money before you go, but exchange rates in Ireland are roughly the same as elsewhere. There's no limit on the amount of money you can take into the country.

## BUDGETING FOR YOUR STAY

Dublin has become one of the most expensive cities in Europe. A hotel room for two will cost at least IR£60/€76 a night, and more likely IR£72-120/€91-152, if you want to stay somewhere with a bit of character. For transport (including airport transfer), expect to spend IR£24/€30 for two people for two days. A pub lunch will cost you around IR£7/€9 per person, while you should expect to pay at least IR£18/€23 for an evening meal. Even if you only have sandwiches or snacks, you won't get away with much less than IR£5/€6.50. A pint of beer costs over IR£2.50/€3. For a two-day, two-night stay, two people should, therefore, expect to spend at least IR£300/€380 (not including flights), and IR£420/€533 on average.

## LOCAL TIME

Ireland conforms to GMT. Clocks go forward in late spring, in line with British Summer Time.

## VOLTAGE

The electric current is 220 volts, and they use standard three-pin plugs. The two-pin shaver sockets in bathrooms can be used to recharge your mobile phone at a pinch, but shouldn't be used for any other electrical appliances.

## SECURITY

Thefts have increased in Dublin in recent years. If you hire a car, don't leave anything in it and avoid carrying photo or video equipment about too obviously in the evening.

## HEALTH

EU citizens should obtain an E111 form from their local post office a few days before departure and will then be entitled to a refund of any medical expenses on their return. In Dublin, everyday medicines (painkillers, throat pastilles, cough mixture, digestive remedies etc.) are on sale across the counter in supermarkets as well as chemists. Emergency care is free and the number to call in an emergency is 999. If you pay for your plane or ferry ticket by credit card, you should be entitled to cover for medical expenses and the cost of repatriation (check before you go). Otherwise, it's best to take out insurance for the cost of repatriation with a reliable insurance company before departure.

## POUNDS, FEET AND INCHES

The changeover to the metric system is taking place slowly in Ireland and you'll still find road signs giving distances or speed limits in miles. Beer is sold in pints and the food in markets is sold in pounds and ounces. If you fall for a traditional tweed fabric, bear in mind that material is measured in feet and inches

### PUBLIC AND BANK HOLIDAYS

- New Year's Day
- St Patrick's Day: 17 March
- Good Friday
- Easter Monday
- First Monday in May
- June Bank Holiday (Irish Republic): first Monday in June
- Battle of the Boyne Day (Northern Ireland): 12 July
- August Bank Holiday: first Monday in August
- October Bank Holiday: last Monday in October
- Christmas Day
- St Stephen's Day (Boxing Day): 26 December

here – forget and you could end up with short curtains or a throw that doesn't cover your sofa completely. There are conversion charts on page 126 to help you when converting from imperial to metric measurements.

# FROM MEGALITHS TO CELTIC ART

Although the Celts occupy only a small part of Irish history, it is their culture that has become most closely associated with the island. Irish monks may have spread the Celtic word far and wide, but the Celtic culture is not the whole story of Irish art.

found at Gleninsheen. Made 700 years before the birth of Christ, it is on display at the National Museum (see p. 51).

### THE FIRST WAVE OF INVADERS

Well before the arrival of the Celts, the island was settled by invaders from Scotland. They were known as the Fir Bolg, and feature in many Irish legends. They left behind great megalithic monuments, such as the one at Newgrange north of Dublin, which show that they followed a complex cult of

the dead, as well as practising a form of astronomy. The objects discovered in the course of archaeological excavations include splendid solid gold necklaces, such as the one

### THE COMING OF THE CELTS

The Celts' profound influence on Ireland is evident in the craft work of the island. Coming from continental Europe, they landed on the island in the 4th century BC. The largest of the Celtic tribes was that of the Gaels, who arrived from Spain (Galicia in particular) and France. These proud warriors domesticated the horse and were expert swordsmen. Their social organization was based on the family and tribe. They formed an egalitarian community, in which women and wordsmiths had a privileged place. Their spiritual world was peopled with gods and heroes who were a lasting source of inspiration for the Irish imagination and its poetry. They also brought with them the beginnings of cuisine, with leavened bread, beer, mead and butter.

### CELTIC MYSTICISM

The Celts practised their religion at the heart of nature, with great open-air festivals throughout the agricultural year. Their gods symbolized the forces of nature, such as the sky, the earth, water, light

and fire. The world of the dead was a reality for them. Death was a passage to another world, parallel to our own but equally real. This may explain their courage in battle. The leading thinkers of their society were druids, learned sages who transmitted their knowledge by word of mouth. The Celtic people had a very precise system of rules

*Glendalough Monastery*

and laws, and titles and power were granted only by means of elections.

## THE GOLDEN AGE

With the fall of the Roman Empire, Europe descended into chaos. Ireland, which was saved from Roman conquest by Julius Caesar, was the last bastion of refined civilization. At the same time, the country's conversion to Christianity began with St Patrick, one of the first missionaries to reach Ireland, in 432. The new church was unable to completely eradicate the heritage of Celtic mysticism and was forced partially to accept it. However, the island was fertile ground for conversion and monasteries began to spring up everywhere. Glendalough monastery, south of Dublin, in the romantic setting of the Wicklow Mountains conservation area, gives an idea of the reclusive life of the first monks, who were among the finest scholars in Europe. In the monasteries, they first used Celtic writing (*ogham*) and later Latin. Their illuminated manuscripts are among the oldest in the world, and include the *Book of Kells,* on display at Trinity College, with sumptuous illuminations including all the interlacing Celtic motifs such as knots, birds

### CELTIC JEWELLERY

As soon as they arrived on the island in the 4th century BC, the Celts began to demonstrate their creative skills by making magnificent jewellery. The most famous piece is the Tara Brooch, on display at the National Museum (see p. 51). It consists of an ornate ring and a pin, and was used to fasten a cloak. The gold jewellery made by the Celts has been a source of inspiration for Irish jewellers since the 19th century.

and dragons (see p. 50). The Christians retained the Celts' social organization, the important place accorded to women, both in the religious communities and elsewhere, and their love of legends, poetry and art. At that time, Ireland was known as the 'island of saints and scholars'. This golden age was cut short at the end of the 8th century by the arrival of the Vikings. The site of Dublin, already occupied by the Celts, soon began to be urbanized by the new colonists.

# WOOL AND TWEED

The story of Irish textiles is one of coarse fabrics and rough, warm wool, dyed in muted, faded hues inspired by the gentle colours of the moors. Wool from Ireland's sheep is transformed into soft pullovers and hard-wearing jackets as well as lengths of cloth that are exported worldwide.

## LOCAL MATERIALS

Since the Bronze Age, the inhabitants of Ireland have known how to spin wool and weave it into fabrics. These became one of the first exports in the Middle Ages. Felted, woven or knitted, wool is used to keep out the cold and rain. Oiled with sheep's fat, it becomes waterproof and weather resistant.

## DONEGAL TWEED

Every part of the island makes a particular tweed in its workshops, but the most famous is the Donegal tweed. The village of Ardara has the greatest concentration of weavers in the land. It was once the site of a large fair to which merchants came from far and wide. The necessary

know-how had been imported from Scotland and England by a rich Englishwoman who wanted to develop the region. Further south in Foxford, in County Mayo, plaids are produced as well as tweeds.

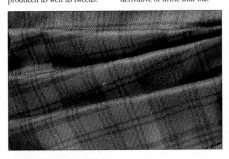

## NATURAL COLOURS

The sheep are sheared in summer and the wool is then washed and dyed with natural pigments obtained from local plants. The granite lichen gives a beautiful dark red, while peat soot produces a brownish-yellow hue. Heather is required for a brighter

yellow, while blackberry roots are needed for brown. Blackthorn, iris and gorse are also used. The dye is fixed with oak tannin, which has replaced the ammoniac derivative of urine that was

formerly used. The craftsmen all have their own secret mixtures with which they create their colours. Once the wool has been dyed, it's spun and wound on the large bobbins that are used on the looms. The types of tweed obtained depend on the kind of weaving.

There are three large families of tweed in Donegal: the herringbones in matching tones, the mottled fabrics picked out with flecks of colour and the tartan blends that are repeats of age-old patterns.

## FISHERMEN'S SWEATERS

Irish knitwear, with its complex stitches, was made famous by the Aran islands. Aran knitwear has almost become a something of a national symbol and is now produced all over Ireland.

The original sweaters were worn by fishermen. The different stitches each have a precise symbolism. The honeycomb is a positive sign referring to the industrious nature of the bee, which is always rewarded for its work. Some say that seeing a swarm of bees before setting sail is a portent of a good catch. The diamond stitches symbolize wealth and success. Cable stitch brings good luck and safety at sea. Basket stitch represents the fisherman's basket full of fish. The double zigzag represents the twists and turns, the high and low points of marriage. The tree of life, with its network of branches, symbolizes the strength of the ancestral line and the unity of the family.

### THE FAMILY BRAND

Put together in an endless series of combinations, the stitching patterns tell a story. On the Aran Islands, each family had its own unique combination, which they

could identify. Women would pass the pattern from one generation to another. Immediately recognizable, it allowed the bloated body of a drowned sailor to be easily identified.

### EVERY ONE UNIQUE

If you find an Aran sweater you love but would prefer it in a different size or colour, you may be in for a disappointment. The hand-knitted jumpers all differ in terms of the stitches used, the colour, or the shape of the neckline. These individual variations give them their charm and make each one quite unique.

# LITERARY DUBLIN

Who would have thought that an island located on the edge of Europe, long deprived of its own language, would become one of the foremost writing nations of the world? Dublin is engaged in a permanent love affair with its men and women of letters, whether serious and literary, or whimsical and poetic. Some were leading lights of literary *salons*, others spent more time propping up one of the city's many bars, but they're all still remembered today.

### THE WAR OF LANGUAGE

Although forced to give up their native tongue, Gaelic, the Irish took up the challenge and have produced some of the greatest writers in the English language, including four Nobel Prize winners, W.B. Yeats (1923), George Bernard Shaw (1925), Samuel Beckett (1969) and Seamus Heaney (1995). These literary giants rejuvenated and revivified writing in the English language by injecting their fantasy, imagination and virtuosity. The Irish love of words isn't restricted to scholars, but is a characteristic of the whole nation. All over the city, from university lecture halls to pubs, Dubliners are never reticent about their passion.

### FROM GULLIVER TO DRACULA

The first famous Irish writer was Jonathan Swift (1667-

*Swift, Gulliver's Travels*

1745), Dean of St Patrick's Cathedral and writer of satirical stories, including his most acclaimed work *Gulliver's Travels*. The fact that *Dracula* was a member of Dublin society is rather less well known. The book's author, Bram Stoker, worked as an official at Dublin Castle. It took him five years to write *Dracula*, much influenced by Celtic legends and an interest in the supernatural.

### EARLY PROVOCATION

If *Dracula* was out of tune with 19th-century literature, another Dublin writer was even more reviled. Oscar Wilde was a brilliant pillar of the most elitist salons and a remarkable playwright, but his provocative attitude and blatant homosexuality cost him his liberty. When he was released from prison, he went

*Oscar Wilde's house*

*Oscar Wilde*

into self-imposed exile in Paris, where he died in poverty. Despite this, he remains one of Dublin's most cherished sons. The humorous statue of him on the edge of Merrion Square (see p. 60), where his family lived, is an affectionate tribute.

## GEORGE BERNARD SHAW AND W.B. YEATS

Following in the footsteps of Wilde, George Bernard Shaw, a Dubliner by birth, went to London to pursue his career. His achievements, in the theatre in particular, won him the Nobel Prize. Although he rarely went back to Ireland, he left a third of his royalties to the National Gallery, where you can see his statue. Probably the most eminent of the Irish authors, and certainly the most engaged in the cultural life of the city, was William Butler Yeats. He came from a family of artists (see the National Gallery, p. 60), and is considered the island's greatest poet. He was passionately interested in the stage and co-founded Dublin's Abbey Theatre.

## THE JOYCEAN REVOLUTION

James Joyce revolutionized the world of letters. The skill of his writing technique and the subversive nature of his work soon made him the target for censure. His novels draw an uncompromising portrait of Dublin society. His masterpiece, *Ulysses*, mirrors the structure of Homer's *Odyssey*, but sets the journey of its hero in the various districts of Dublin. Joyce is so idolized by Dubliners that a public holiday has been created to allow people to

celebrate him in style. Bloomsday, on 16 June, is named after Leopold Bloom, the hero of *Ulysses*. On that day, a walking tour allows fans of Joyce to follow in his footsteps and visit all the places mentioned in the novel (see p. 21). After moving to Paris, Joyce became friends with another gifted Irishman, Samuel Beckett, who was a native of Dublin. Hounded from the island by censorship, the young playwright achieved fame in France with plays such as *Waiting for Godot*. A number of Dublin sites can be identified in his work.

## IN WITH THE NEW

The capital's great literary tradition is still very much alive, with modern writers bearing tender and humorous witness to life in Ireland. The best-known of them is Roddy Doyle, whose work inspired the trilogy of films *The Commitments*, *The Snapper* and *The Van*, while his novel *Paddy Clarke Ha Ha Ha* won the prestigious Booker Prize. Dubliners Joseph O'Connor and Colm Tóibín are gradually achieving the same sort of fame. Like John McGahern and Edna O'Brien before them, they belong to a generation of high-quality writers born or based in the island.

## ALCOHOLIC INSPIRATION

Many other playwrights, essayists and short-story writers have left their mark here and there in the city. They include J.M. Synge, Patrick Kavanagh, Flann O'Brien (whose real name was Brian Nolan) and Brendan Behan. Known for their inexhaustable appetite for alcohol, their ghosts still haunt the smoky pubs where they first found their inspiration.

*Statue of Patrick Kavanagh*

# BEER AND WHISKEY

It wouldn't be right to visit Ireland without sampling some of the national specialities. The most famous is undoubtedly Guinness but it's far from being the only one. Irish whiskey makers pride themselves on producing a tipple that's at least as good as its Scottish rival. See what you think.

### THE MOST FAMOUS STOUT

In Dublin, where brewing has provided a living for hundreds of families, Guinness rules supreme, with a daily production of 4 million pints. Anyone who has never tasted this type of beer, which is also known as stout or porter, should try some here. Purists will tell you it doesn't travel well and is best drunk close to where it's brewed. If Guinness is the best known of the Irish beers, with its black colour and creamy white head, there are others, such as Murphy's and Beamish (stouts), that are milder and smoother. They are more common in the south of the country. As well as stout, there are ales such as Smithwicks, and lagers such as Harp.

### MANUFACTURING SECRETS

Beer is made from barley. Part of the grain provides the malt, while the other part is roasted, giving the beer its brown colour. The bitter taste comes from the hops that are added during the manufacturing process, then the beer is left to mature in huge vats. But that's not the end of it. A good pint of Guinness must be drawn very slowly, then left to allow the bubbles to rise and form a pale head on the dark liquid. The glass is then topped up to the brim. The whole process takes about three minutes. If the beer is pulled properly, the head retains the mark of the drinker's lips to the end and leaves a series of rings around the glass.

### POSTERS AND SLOGANS

Guinness is famous both in Ireland and abroad, partly because of its distinctive taste, but also as the result of a series of clever publicity campaigns, at a time when advertising was still in its infancy. The catchy slogans 'Guinness is good for you' and 'My Goodness! My Guinness!' were so effective in persuading consumers that the drink was good for their health that Guinness was even recommended for undersized children and nursing mothers. Many bars used the advertising posters to decorate their windows or walls. If you want to find out

## THE LEADING BRANDS

Three major distilleries have long shared the production of whiskey: Dublin, Midleton in County Cork, and Bushmills in Northern Ireland. In the face of Scottish competition, they have amalgamated and now operate under the Pernod-Ricard umbrella, while retaining their different brands to provide something for everyone. Bushmills is the oldest whiskey in the world, dating from 1608, and Bushmills Malt is much appreciated by connoisseurs. Powers is rarely exported, and makes a good souvenir (IR£15/€19). Twelve-year-old Jameson Gold Specia lReserve, Joyce's favourite brand, is a top-quality whiskey (IR£37/€47). Paddy's is much lighter and is good for mixing.

more about these innovative campaigns, a visit to the Guinness Hop Store is a must (see p. 71).

## THE RED GOLD OF THE BARRELS

Ireland's other famous drink is whiskey (spelt with an 'e' when it's Irish or American, without when it's Scotch). It was already around at the time of the Celts, known as *uisce beatha* – 'water of life'. This later became *fuisce* in the language of the Norman invaders, before being anglicized as 'whiskey'. The ingredients are barley, water and yeast. The barley grains are dried, sorted, soaked and malted. After fermentation, the wort is distilled three times in succession, which progressively purifies the alcohol (Scotch whisky is only distilled twice). The liquid is then passed into a heated still, where it's vaporized before condensing to form a distillate. The last distillation produces whiskey, which is stored in oak barrels to age for 3-15 years.

## PORTER CAKE AND HOT TODDIES

Stout and whiskey are also used in a number of Irish recipes. To make porter cake, a deliciously rich traditional tea-time treat, dried fruit is steeped in stout.

When you're in a pub, ask for an Irish coffee, a delicious mixture of whiskey and strong coffee topped with cream, or a hot toddy, made from whiskey flavoured with lemon and cloves. When you're in a sweet shop, try whiskey-flavoured toffee of truffles.

## THE NEW DESIGNERS

Dublin once had the reputation of being the old-fashioned capital of a poor rural island. But, with the boom in the economy and its worldwide renown in music and film, Dublin is now considered one of Europe's 'hippest' cities, with an astonishing number of international designers in relation to its population size.

### LOOKING TO AMERICA

Sybil Connolly was one of the first Irish designers to achieve international fame, using Celtic influences with horizontally pleated linen and fine Irish crochet. America took her to its heart, and Jacqueline Kennedy became an enthusiastic client (one of the White House portraits shows her in a Sybil Connolly ballgown). Connolly also designed ceramics for Tiffany's from her elegant Georgian home in Merrion Square. While later designers continued to make an impact in America, it was not until the arrival of Paul Costelloe that the London fashion world began to sit up and take notice.

### COSTELLOE, THE GROUND-BREAKER

Paul Costelloe's achievement has been a compromise between traditional wearable

clothes and a more international look. Moving away from old-fashioned florals and frills, he places the accent on good cut and a timeless, understated style. He uses traditional tweeds but

gives them structured shapes and pure lines. After gaining experience in London, Milan and New York, he launched his own line in 1979, with immediate success. His suits found favour with the late Princess Diana, and Mary Robinson, former president of Ireland and Liza Minnelli also rank amongst his customers. He remains an important figure in the world of Irish fashion.

### JOHN ROCHA LINEN

With fellow success story Louise Kennedy, this innovative Dublin designer of Chinese and Portuguese descent has played a major part in the Irish renaissance. Voted designer of the year in London in 1993, he's known for the simple cut of his clothes. Subtly influenced by his Asian heritage, he favours pure lines and respects his raw materials. He uses linen successfully,

## AMAZING BAGS

Look out for great bags by Orla Kiely and Helen Cody. Kiely's innovative chic collection features stripes, spots and craft cross-stitch on leather and funky materials. A Helen Cody bag – usually in the shape of a fish or a flower – is a one-off collector's item. Original pieces are available by both designers at the Kilkenny Centre (see p. 87).

and his fluid, cleverly unstructured outfits seem to slim the silhouette. Although he makes no secret of the fact that he prefers lanky models, his designs suit everyone. His strength lies in his simple

but clever cutting, hand painting on fabrics and inspired embellishment. More recently, he has been involved in interior decoration, creating lines for Waterford Crystal and designing hotels, such as the Dublin Morrison (see p. 75).

## THE EXTRAORDINARY LAINEY KEOGH

This former laboratory technician has had an unusual career. In 1983, she knitted a jumper for a friend who was a producer for the rock band U2. Bono and the rest of the group fell in love with it, and the self-taught young designer was promoted to the rank of dresser to the stars. Now adored by the leading Hollywood players, she counts Demi Moore and Isabella Rossellini among her clients. Naomi Campbell, who models Keogh's more unusual pieces, set tongues wagging in Puritan Ireland by stepping onto the catwalk in an asymmetrical knitted dress that almost bared one of her breasts. Knitwear is a fantastic medium for Lainey Keogh. She mixes wool and cashmere with plastic, sequins, metal and new

materials to create elegant, figure-hugging compositions that are comfortable to wear (see p. 86-87).

## THE FANTASTIC HATS OF PHILIP TREACY

This is the place for hat-lovers as Philip Treacy's creations are works of art owing more to sculpture than millinery. He has claimed to be inspired by the complicated structure and vast scale of Cologne cathedral, and the greatest names in fashion have latched on to his talent. Karl Lagerfeld, John Galliano, Victor Edelstein, Valentino and Alexander McQueen have all used his hats for their shows. In Dublin, you can find Philip Treacy hats at Brown Thomas and Debenhams.

## FESTIVALS AND FUN

Hand-in-hand with the Irish love of laughter and music goes an ever-present sense of celebration, expressed, more often than not, in simple, inexpensive pleasures. The big religious festivals, ancient Celtic traditions, horse-racing and other sports all provide the Irish with the opportunity to go out, drink and have fun.

### ST PATRICK'S DAY

The Irish national holiday is celebrated on 17 March in honour of the saint who converted the island to Christianity in the 5th century. In Dublin, St Patrick is now the subject of Ireland's biggest annual celebration, with three days of music, dance, street parades and spectacular fireworks. Many Irish exiles take the opportunity to come back to the island, adding to the exuberance of the atmosphere. It's all much more low-key in the provinces, where it's still mainly a religious celebration. In the morning, the Irish go to Mass wearing shamrocks in their buttonholes. St Patrick's Day really owes its fame to the United States, and New York in particular, where the descendants of Irish immigrants have turned it into a gigantic festival, complete with marches and parades.

### DUBLIN THEATRE FESTIVAL

Dublin's rich literary heritage is splendidly experienced each autumn in the Dublin Theatre Festival. It runs for the first two weeks in October, complemented by a three week fringe festival which starts in the last week of September. The Theatre Festival ranks along with Edinburgh as the leading theatrical event in these islands, featuring both international and home-grown talent. Drama, music, mime, dance, puppetry and street theatre abound. The beauty is that all the venues are within walking distance of the city centre. The Fringe festival is equally lively, with a mix of theatre, dance, comedy and the visual arts at over 20 venues citywide. Pre- and après-theatre keep the excitement going either side of performances. All in all, this is a great way to see Dublin at play! (See also p. 118.)

### THE RACES

The races are also an opportunity to celebrate. People at every level of society in Ireland love gambling. Race meetings last several days,

providing the opportunity for family get-togethers and holidays. In Dublin, the horse-racing season takes the public to all the racecourses in the surrounding area, especially neighbouring County Kildare, which is an important centre of racehorse breeding. People are also passionately interested in showjumping. The main event, the Kerrygold Horse

Show, takes place in Dublin at the start of August. One of the days culminates in a dress parade, when a prize is given to the best-dressed woman and, above all, to the one wearing the best hat. The pubs around the racecourses are kept busy, of course, and the atmosphere is hard to describe. For the less affluent, greyhound racing provides the same kind of excitement for a more modest price. Just as many people gamble on the dogs, though the bets start at only 50p/€0.63.

## SPORT

The Irish are passionate about sport in general and team sports in particular. Even though spectators can get very worked up and the beer flows freely, the atmosphere is always good-natured. On finals days,

Dublin is invaded by crowds of fans dressed from head to foot in their team colours, and souvenir shops overflow with jerseys, hats and scarves so that people can express their support. The most popular sports are hurling (a kind of forerunner of field hockey which is played on grass with goals similar to those used in rugby), Gaelic

football (a combination of football and rugby) and rugby itself (Ireland's Six Nations matches are always worth seeing, either live from the stands or on TV with a pint or two in one of the pubs). Dublin has one of the three best Gaelic football teams in the country, and the capital turns into one giant fan club whenever they play.

## TRADITIONAL MUSIC

One of Ireland's most striking characteristics is the constant sound of music – in Dublin's streets, in the pubs, wherever you go, you'll always hear someone singing or playing. Whether it's a guitarist humming a ballad, *a cappella* singing in Gaelic, or someone playing the flute or concertina, the same tunes come up again and again, and everyone seems to know them.

### A LIVING TRADITION

Ireland has always remained firmly attached to its culture as a means of resisting colonial influence. Like the Celtic legends, Irish music has been handed down from generation to generation,

often as a symbol of national pride. Originally, the melodies were not written down, but were passed on orally, as was the skill of playing musical instruments. Children learnt to play instinctively by watching their elders. In the streets of Dublin, you'll see plenty of children performing without inhibition. Although

Irish traditional music may appear to have changed little during the last century, it has successfully evolved to embrace outside influences, without losing its own identity. Well known bands such as Altan mix rock and Irish folk music, Kíla combine traditional music with rap whilst the Afro Celt Sound System offer a heady dance mix of Celtic and West African musical styles and instruments.

### IRISH INSTRUMENTS

Initially the Celts only used derivatives of the drum to make music, including the

*bodhrán* (pronounced 'borarn'), which is still widely used today. A frame drum with

a goatskin head, it is struck with a stick or the hands to produce a variety of warm sounds. The harp, an instrument that appears frequently in Celtic legend,

American folk music in the 1960s. Finally, the *uilleann* pipes, once used to encourage warriors to fight, are still used today to accompany marching regiments. Similar in sound to the Scottish bagpipes, although less harsh, the main difference is that the air pressure is controlled with the elbows rather than the lungs.

grander scale, the *fleadh* (pronounced 'fla'), is a big musical gathering or festival. Singing is also an important part of Irish music, whatever the occasion. The complex traditional vocal style known as *sean-nós* is particularly beautiful. The songs, sung unaccompanied in the Irish language, typically convey stories of love, hope and oppression as well as embracing revolutionary or political ideals.

## ADD TO YOUR CD COLLECTION

If you're looking for classics, go for an album by the Chieftains (*Chieftains Four*), one by De Dannan and another by Altan *(Island Angel)*. Though now disbanded, The Bothy Band *(Old Hag, You Have Killed Me)* and Clannad *(Macalla)* shouldn't be overlooked. If you like ballads, listen to the unforgettable Christy Moore. For newer styles, try Kílá *(Tóg E Go Bóg É)*, Goats Don't Shave or the Afro Celt Sound System.

## SESSIONS

During a *seisiún,* or session, several musicians come together to perform traditional music. If it's an informal occasion, the artists learn to play together by improvising.

is less popular today, though it was very fashionable in Irish drawing-rooms in the 17th and 18th centuries. Flutes, on the other hand, including the good old tin whistle, a cheap instrument that's relatively easy to learn, are vital to the lively jigs and reels you'll hear in the pubs. With the *bodhrán* and fiddle, they form the basis of the traditional group. The concertina is another popular instrument, as are the spoons, which are used to provide rhythmic accompaniment. The guitar and banjo arrived later with the rebirth of

Such sessions are very popular in Dublin pubs, especially at Sunday lunchtimes. On a

## SET DANCING

The Irish love dance and much of Ireland's traditional music was originally written to accompany dancing. Set dancing consists of a number of traditional set figures, with the dancers changing partners in the course of the dance. The music is played by a *céilí* band, the most famous of which come from County Clare, in the west of Ireland. To find out more, visit the excellent Ceol, the museum of traditional music (see p. 70), or keep an eye (or an ear) out for news of traditional evenings in Dublin.

# IRISH ROCK

Known worldwide through groups such as U2 and The Cranberries, the Irish rock scene is one of the most dynamic in the world. Given the size of the country, the number of Irish artists to have achieved world fame is astonishing.

## FROM FOLK TO ROCK

Two factors have opened the way to this burgeoning of talent: the Irish love of music and the close ties formed

between the United States and Ireland by immigration. In the 1960s and 70s, the folk music revival created new opportunities for Irish artists and traditional sounds influenced American singers such as Bob Dylan and Joan Baez. Some members of this first wave of musicians, such as the Clancy Brothers, the Dubliners and Christy Moore, stuck to folk, while others turned to rock. In the 1970s, one of these musicians, Van Morrison, managed to combine elements from the Celtic heritage with the rhythms of rock and blues. Rory Gallagher, who was born in Donegal, took a similar path.

## PUNK SHOCK

The punk movement, which arrived in London with the Sex Pistols, spread quickly to Northern Ireland, where it symbolized revolt against the moral order advocated by the puritan Protestant churches. In Dublin, the punk movement was less active, and only the Boomtown Rats, under Bob Geldof, have left any lasting memory. However, traditional music with a punk flavour

*Graffiti on the walls of the Windmill Lane studios*

led to the international success of the Pogues, an Irish band who emigrated to London. New to the scene are the Subtonics, part of the new pop-punk trend.

## THE ETERNAL U2

Since the late 1980s, Dublin has produced a number of well-known rock bands, including the Virgin Prunes, and of course the legendary U2, led by singer Bono. U2 have proved to be Ireland's best musical export, achieving the same sort of fame as their predecessors, the Rolling Stones. U2 became to Dublin what the Beatles were to Liverpool. They bought The Kitchen club and turned it into one of the centres of Dublin rock. Their worldwide hit, *Sunday, Bloody Sunday*, about the troubles in Northern Ireland, gave a political dimension to their work. There has been an explosion of creativity in their wake, and now there are over 5,000 rock groups in the island (and 1,200 in Dublin alone). Some of them, such as Ash, from Ulster, are even beginning to compete with the big boys.

## A DYNAMIC ROCK SCENE

The Cranberries are immensely popular in a slightly different vein, with their own brand of rock producing a decidedly Celtic flavour. Their lead singer, Dolores O'Riordan, is considered to be one of the finest female voices in the business. Another influential singer, Sinéad O'Connor, has also had huge success as

groups include The Corrs and My Bloody Valentine, though there are plenty of newcomers hoping to steal the limelight. Young Irish musicians often go to London in search of international recognition, though Dublin remains one of the most fertile breeding grounds for popular music. The three young members of JJ72 seem to be the favourites of the musical press at the moment. The group One Minute Silence, led by Brian Barry, is more oriented towards metal rap, giving a traditional slant to the Iron Maiden and Led Zeppelin styles. The best places to listen to new generation bands are the clubs *Lillies Bordello*, *Vicar Street* and *Eamon Doran's*.

### ROCK AND STROLL

Enthusiastic rock fans can make their way around the city in the footsteps of their idols. Ask for the *Rock and Stroll* leaflet at the tourist information office. It contains a detailed list of 16 legendary sites, such as the Windmill Lane studios where U2 recorded their first record, and the Bad Ass Café where Sinéad O'Connor made a living as a waitress. If you'd rather go on a guided tour, it will take up two hours of your time and cost you IR£5/€6.35 per person.

## BOY (AND GIRL) BAND FEVER

In the specialist category of boy bands, Boyzone reign supreme, following a meteoric rise to fame at home and abroad. Following hard on their heels, Westlife and Mytown are adored by teens and tweenies alike, while B*witched do it for Irish girl power.

well as ruffling a few feathers with her outspoken views on religion. Other popular

# RETRACING THE REVOLUTION

When the Irish republic was proclaimed in 1949, at the end of a slow process of independence, the country had been in a state of rebellion for four centuries, lurching from crisis to crisis. Dublin has not forgotten its revolutionary past.

*The Bank of Ireland*

## FOREIGN ALLIES

When the Protestant landowners first began to colonize the country, the rebellion of the Irish found its inspiration in religious differences. The Catholics called for help from the Spanish and French, who were always ready to fight the English. Their attempts failed, isolating Dublin and the surrounding region, which then came under British rule.

century was a period of violent repression as the English extended their power throughout the country. The aggression of the British troops and the harshness of the landowners led to unrest.

## REVOLUTIONARY FERVOUR

With the end of the 18th century, the Irish rebels were inspired by events in France and America. Catholics did not have the right to vote, own

Irishmen. It failed, but the terrified Anglo-Irish Protestants moved the Parliament, then housed in what is now the Bank of Ireland (see p. 47), from Dublin to London.

## THE AWAKENING OF THE NATIONAL CONSCIOUSNESS

In 1828, a Member of Parliament from the west of Ireland, Daniel O'Connell, known as 'the Liberator', organized a peaceful rebellion in support of Catholic rights. Just when events seemed to be turning in its favour, the Great Famine struck. It decimated the population, with at least a million Irish people dying, and around 1·5 million being forced to emigrate. The English government's role in

*Charles Stewart Parnell before Parliament*

## OPPRESSIVE RULE

The island was at first divided into two zones. Fortifications known as the *Pale* (from the word 'palisade') were raised all around Dublin and the Gaelic Irish had to prove that they came in peace before being allowed to cross it – hence the expression 'living beyond the Pale'. The 18th

land or to have an education. In Dublin, economic development brought new ideas and fostered a climate of rebellion. In 1796, sympathizers came from France to help the rebels, but their efforts were in vain. Two years later, an attempted overthrow was orchestrated by the Dubliner Wolfe Tone and his United

*Charles Stewart Parnell*

*Daniel O'Connell*

the crisis increased the sense of revolt among the Irish. Working alongside the Catholic movements, Protestant Charles Stewart Parnell negotiated a form of autonomy, Home Rule, and harnessed the emerging forces of nationalism.

## THE EASTER REBELLION

In spite of a number of political concessions, the Catholics remained desperately poor. Dublin was an over-populated and unsanitary city. In 1913, James Larkin (see p. 43) and James Connolly launched a general strike and founded the Irish Citizen Army. The strikers were forced to capitulate, but the rebellion took its course. A revolution

was planned for Easter 1916. The headquarters was the General Post Office in O'Connell Street (see p. 42), and various strategic objectives, such as the Four Courts (see p. 49) and St Stephen's Green (see p. 58), were targeted. A thousand volunteers came forward, and Patrick Pearse proclaimed the Republic. The British troops suppressed the insurrection

*James Larkin*

in a bloodbath, and most of the rebel leaders were killed. In the 1918 election, Eamon De Valera and Michael Collins, under the banner of Sinn

(see p. 42) ... (see p. 49) ... (see p. 58) ... (see p. 43)

### STRONG ROOTS

It was in the 19th century that the Irish began to show an interest in their Celtic heritage and acquired a national consciousness. The Gaelic language and culture were reborn and a number of traditional sports associations sprang up. National pride is still expressed very much through these mediums, which explains why music and sport are so important for the Irish.

Fein, founded in 1905, won 75% of the seats. But the difficulties were exacerbated by acts of terrorism. An Anglo-Irish treaty was finally signed in 1921, conceding relative independence to only 26 counties, which constituted the Free State, leaving those in the north under English rule. Civil war again broke out, sealing the partition between the two Irelands. The Irish Republican Army (IRA) refused to lay down its arms, began a terrorist resistance and increased its attacks on English property. The Republic of Ireland was finally declared in 1949.

*Four Courts*

## CRYSTAL AND CHINA

The English colonists brought a whole new way of life. Their drawing rooms and dining tables were adorned with delicate porcelain and ornate cut-crystal glassware, and the manufacture of these desirable items soon became part of the Irish heritage. The new factories found a natural home in a land renowned for the skill and art of its craftwork.

### WATERFORD CRYSTAL

The Waterford Crystal factory was founded in 1783 to the south of Dublin. Despite an international reputation, economic conditions forced it to close in 1851. Nearly a century later, in 1947, it was reopened, and master glassmakers and engravers were brought from continental Europe to train the local workforce. The glassblower's skill lies in obtaining a regular thickness of glass that the engravers and cutters can work on. The factory is now the largest of its kind in the world, and one of the most prestigious. It specializes in cut and engraved crystal (vases, candelabra and chandeliers), traditionally very ornate in style, though the designer John Rocha has recently created a more understated line. As a result of Waterford's success, other glassworks have sprung up in Galway, Cavan and, above all, Tipperary, where the fashion designer Louise Kennedy has successfully tried her hand at contemporary design.

## CHINA BASKETS

Ireland's best-known porcelain factory is at Belleek, in Northern Ireland. Its founder used the resources of his lands (clay, kaolin, feldspar and schist) to manufacture china known as *parian* ware, which imitated Paros marble. The factory's speciality today is the

later decorated with exquisite porcelain flowers. Gum arabic is added to the slip (the fluid clay used to cast the pieces) to obtain a material that's sufficiently malleable. Generally, the pieces are made by men and then decorated by women. The result is slightly old-fashioned, but the Belleek

production of fine china baskets that are surprisingly light and almost transparent. The craftsmen who make them are highly skilled. After preparing the narrow strips of clay that will form the baskets, they weave them like basket makers, producing delicate receptacles that are

factory has many devoted admirers. In a simpler style, Donegal Parian China, with its less elaborate basket designs, is made very close to Belleek, in Ballyshannon, Donegal.

## DRESDEN IN IRELAND

The delicate Dresden figurines that are known worldwide carry on a tradition imported from Germany. Descendants of the craft's founder came to live in Ireland,

near Limerick. Here they make reproductions of traditional designs, such as little figures in 18th-century costume, decked out in china lace. The figurines are cast in moulds, then the various parts are assembled before a first firing at 900°C/1,650°F. The lace dresses that look so fragile are made from tuile that's soaked in slip, then delicately draped or gathered to form frills and furbelows. Glazed, then fired for a second time at 1,300°C/2,370°F, the tuile disintegrates, leaving only china lace that's ready for painting and decorating before the third and final firing.

# CELTIC KITSCH

Among the souvenirs and gifts which flood Dublin's shops and markets, you'll find a number of recurring motifs which have their roots in Celtic mythology or ancient customs. These days, too many are mass-produced in the Far East, but kitsch is still part of Irish culture.

### THE SHAMROCK

The shamrock, or cloverleaf, appears on almost everything in Ireland, from sports shirts to planes, although it isn't a very ancient symbol. In fact the shamrock has only been used as the national emblem since the 17th century. Legend has it that St Patrick used it to illustrate the Holy Trinity, but the true success of the trefoil dates only from the Gaelic revival of the 19th century, when a number of nationalist associations began to use it in earnest.

### THE HERO'S HARP

The official Irish national emblem is the harp, which figures on banknotes and coins. Guinness also uses it on its logo, and it's often printed on caps and T-shirts in the national colours. In

fact, it's not an instrument that's commonly used in popular music, as it doesn't lend itself to the rhythms of the dances and drinking songs. But it does has a association with one of the heroes of Irish history, Brian Boru, who was an accomplished harpist, as well as King of Munster and high king of Ireland in the 11th century. He defeated the Vikings in a historic battle, and the harp indirectly became the symbol of resistance to invasion. The harp on display at Trinity College is said to be have belonged to him (although it's thought to date from the 14th century, see p. 50).

## THE SHILLELAGH

Found in every souvenir and gift shop, the shillelagh is in reality nothing more that a piece of twisted blackthorn branch that's passed off to tourists as an ancient weapon. In truth, such branches may well have been used by country people as a walking stick or crook, and brandished occasionally by them during friendly confrontations at fairs and markets.

## THE MISCHIEVOUS WORLD OF THE LEPRECHAUN

The leprechaun turns up everywhere in Ireland, perched, mischievous and grinning, at the end of a rainbow, wearing a green hat and carrying a pot of gold.

The 'little people' of fairy tales and legends, leprechauns are cobblers to the fairies and guardians of their treasure. As the rainbow is supposed to show humans where to find their gold, the poor leprechauns are kept busy, which is probably what makes them look so grumpy. Unlike fairies, who live in merry little communities, the leprechaun lives by himself.

## ST BRIGID'S CROSS

The cross of St Brigid is made of reeds plaited in various patterns. The much-venerated Brigid has an important role in this rural country, as the protector of animals and livestock. She's celebrated on the feast day of Imbolg, which falls on 1 February, at a time of year when animals are most exposed to bad weather. Like all Celtic festivals, it's linked to the cycles of nature, and marks the preparations for sowing. Ireland's national television company, RTE, has made St Brigid's Cross its emblem, and a fine collection of crosses is on display in the annexe of the National Museum at Collins Barracks (see p. 70).

## THATCHED COTTAGES

The postcards and models on sale in Dublin shops set out to convince you that the Irish all live in picturesque thatched cottages. While this was the case for centuries, they're now quite rare.

In days gone by, the cottages were small, long and low, with narrow doors and small windows to keep out the weather. The straw or reed roofs were held in place by fishing nets attached to the masonry with large nails. Although they're now disappearing, they're still one of the island's popular symbols.

## PUB PLEASURES

For many visitors, Dublin's main attraction is its pubs. Pub life is one of the more appealing aspects of the city's heritage and the best place to meet all sorts of local people. As you make your way about the city,

allow for plenty of pub stops, but keep an eye on your alcohol intake if you want to be able to find your way home.

### A HOME FROM HOME

Pubs are a way of life in Ireland. Originally they were almost exclusively frequented by men, who went to their local to meet friends, hear the latest news, put the world to rights and, sometimes, just to get away from the wife and kids. Much has changed in recent years, and pubs now welcome almost as many women as men. The Irish do little in the way of entertaining at home, and friends, family and work colleagues all use the pub for socializing. The atmosphere is often calm and quiet, and people indulge their love of words, a very important pastime in Ireland. Most of the Irish writers are still remembered in their favourite

pubs. Here and there, amid the bottles and advertisements, you'll read quotations or extracts from poems that demonstrate the barman's love of literature.

### MUSIC AND *CRAIC*

Pubs aren't just a place to drink, they're a complete form of leisure activity, with people coming together to make music, sing, laugh and talk. This is what the Irish call the *craic,* a word that means relaxing and generally having fun. Not all pubs offer live music. Where there is music, it's often on certain nights of the week, and styles of music vary considerably, from traditional to folk to rock. To find out what's on, ask around or look out for posters on the walls.

### PANELLING AND MIRRORS

In Dublin, the pubs are part of the architectural heritage. Some of them are several hundred years old, but even the most recent have acquired a patina of nicotine stains and peat soot from the open fires. The finest have dark oak or mahogany panelling and sometimes individual booths for privacy.

Other notable features include marble bar tops, Victorian-style stained glass and, above all, a large number of engraved mirrors. These mirrors were originally designed to advertise the various brands of alcohol.

Some of them are very intricate and quite beautiful. A pub is intended as a haven of peace, and it isn't done to be seen drinking from the street. The view through the front windows is therefore often obscured by frosted glass or a series of shelves. The charm of the interior is only revealed once you step inside.

## PUB DOS AND DON'TS

An authentic Dublin pub is a place where people come to talk. Savour the atmosphere for a few minutes before trying to settle in. Keep an eye out for valuable bar space and move up as soon as someone moves. You are more likely to get in on a conversation if you are at the bar than if you are stuck away in a corner or the no-man's land of mid-floor space. Don't try to force your way into a conversation. Sooner or later, if you make enough eye contact and laugh at enough jokes, someone will address a remark to you. Although they

project a sophisticated veneer, Dubliners actually are still quite inquisitive about foreigners. Only offer to buy a round if someone has bought you a drink first. Don't tell Irish jokes - only the Irish are allowed tell Irish jokes in Ireland! Do not tip

the barman - it's not expected. Don't spend the whole night nursing a half pint, and do not refer to half pint measures as such. A half pint is known as 'a glass'. Finally, *Slainte!* (pronounced 'slawn cha'), is the Irish for 'Good Health'!

### DRINKING-UP TIME

This wonderful Irish institution is the period which follows the official closing time. The call for 'last orders' does not stop your last order being a multiple one! There's nothing to prevent you ordering several pints at once to make it last. And, as the notion of rushing a pint is anathema to the Irish, they have created 'Drinking-up Time' – a twilight period between 'closing time' and when the pub actually closes!

# GEORGIAN ARCHITECTURE

One of the key features of the city of Dublin is its architectural unity, created during what some regard as its golden age. The most elegant buildings and squares date from the reign of George III, when Dublin was in the hands of the Anglo-Protestant ruling class.

## FROM PLANTATIONS TO DOMINATION

The colonization by the Anglo-Norman Catholics was originally largely peaceful. But with the Reformation, English domination went hand-in-hand with religious conflict between those who owed allegiance to the Crown and the new religion, and the Gaels and others of Anglo-Norman extraction who wanted to remain Catholic. These supported the pretenders who opposed the Queen of England, Elizabeth I. The colonial wars began and, with the so-called 'plantations', with lands that were taken away from the Irish Catholics and given to Anglo-Protestants in recognition of their support. The English rule hardened, and Ireland found itself under an iron yoke. The towns grew and trade developed. In the reign of George III, in the 18th century, Dublin, which was then in the hands of the Protestants, entered its golden age.

*George III*

## MONUMENTS, PARKS AND DOORS

The elite of Anglo-Protestant society owned the land and

occupied all the important positions. They wanted a city that reflected their English roots and refinement. The result was the Georgian streets and squares of the

city, of which some elegant vestiges still remain. They were inspired by Classical Antiquity, with geometrical rigour and an almost austere uniformity relieved with decorative details. Much use was made of pediments,

columns, friezes and mouldings. In England, the most famous exponent of the style was Inigo Jones, who took his inspiration from the Florentine architect Andrea Palladio. In Dublin, Custom House (see p. 46), Four Courts (see p. 49) and the Bank of Ireland (see p. 47) were built

in part by Jones's counterpart, James Gandon, who was very fashionable at the time. The squares are another aspect of this urbanization, with tall, virtually identical brick houses standing around green English-style gardens. Merrion Square (see p. 60), Fitzwilliam Square and St Stephen's Green (see p. 59), which are among the finest in the city, are where the gentry would take their walks. Lastly, the rows of terraced houses, distinguishable only by their doors, are another characteristic feature of the Georgian city. These brightly painted doors, with their elegant fanlights, are among the most enduring images of Dublin.

## A TYPICAL TOWNHOUSE

Among the most famous Georgian houses in Dublin is the one belonging to Hugh Lane, now a modern art museum (see p. 45). Its elegance is typical of the large townhouses. The hall and staircase, with their columns and mouldings, are particularly fine.

### ELEGANT GEORGIAN HOUSES

The tall houses were built on several floors. The basement was reserved for the kitchen and pantry, occasionally with a room for the housekeeper. The ground floor was reached by steps flanked by wrought-iron railings. The roads were very muddy in the 18th century, and some of the houses still have the old shoe-scraper next to their front door. The best reception room was found on the first floor – either an elegant

dining room or an imposing drawing room with a high ceiling and decorative stuccoes. From the outside, this hierarchy can be seen in the size of the windows and the complicated balconies adorning them. On the second floor were the master bedrooms (separate rooms for both husband and wife), the bathroom and the lady's boudoir. Higher still were the nursery and the adjacent nanny's room, while the servants were housed in the attic.

## COUNTRY FLAVOURS

In recent years, Dublin has become a cosmopolitan city, with increasing numbers of ethnic and international restaurants. However, if you prefer to eat more traditional dishes, many of the city's pubs still serve hearty local dishes in a warm, convivial atmosphere. Don't expect great inventiveness, only simple, nourishing dishes that are the legacy of more difficult times.

### IN THE BEGINNING THERE WAS THE POTATO...

For a long time Ireland was a very poor country, where the people had only the most basic food to eat. Their diet consisted of little meat and, above all, lots of potatoes. Irish stew is largely comprised of them, while other dishes, such as boxty, contain little else. This Donegal speciality is a kind of thick pancake made of grated potatoes, cooked on a griddle and sometimes stuffed. Potatoes were such a staple of the Irish diet that the potato blight of the mid-1800s caused famine and appalling suffering.

### ... THEN CAME THE CABBAGE

The second most popular staple was the cabbage. Before the cultivated cabbage was imported in the 17th century, wild cabbage and sea-kale were used to make stews and other dishes. One of Ireland's best-known meals is colcannon (a mixture of mashed potatoes and cabbage, milk, butter and onions). It's now mainly served as an accompaniment, but was once widely eaten on lean days, such as Fridays and Halloween, when meat supplies had run out. Cabbage is also a major component of the national dish of bacon and cabbage, which is served on festive occasions, such as St Patrick's Day.

### FARM-PRODUCED MEAT

The rearing of sheep and pigs dates back to Celtic times in Ireland. The meats most commonly eaten and used in traditional recipes were mutton and pork. Irish stew, the national dish, is

## A HEARTY BREAKFAST

If you're used to only having a slice of toast and quick cup of coffee in the morning, you'd better prepare yourself for a sumptuous traditional breakfast (often included in the accommodation tariff). Start with orange juice, then a bowl of porridge or cereal. Next comes a 'fry', consisting of bacon (always known as 'rashers' in Dublin), sausages, black and white pudding, fried egg and tomatoes. This is sometimes accompanied by the traditional Ulster potato cake made with flour and potato and cooked on a hot griddle. Don't worry about the cholesterol – the 'fry' is, in fact, usually grilled these days!

made from potatoes, onions, herbs, and diced mutton cooked slowly in the oven in stock. In more affluent areas, carrots may also be added.

## FISH AND IRISH PREJUDICE

Fish isn't a staple food in Ireland, which is odd given the fact that it's an island. Apart from fish and chips, and the traditional 'fish on Friday', it doesn't figure much in family meals. However, more and more restaurants offer it on their menus, though the Irish themselves don't go for it much. This may be because fish was once considered poor man's fare in Ireland.

Herring and mackerel were sold on the streets of Dublin by Molly Malone (see p. 53) and her colleagues. Salmon, the quintessential Irish fish, was considered a luxury in Celtic times when it was served grilled with honey. Later, it became so common that workers' demands included a request for it to be served no more than three times a week! Nowadays, salmon is eaten everywhere – marinated, smoked, in a sauce, poached or grilled. But oak-smoked wild salmon is the tastiest.

## TEA OR COFFEE

A by-product of the Celtic Tiger economy has been the enormous surge in the popularity of coffee. Until recently, the only choice tended to be whether you took it white or black. Now a proliferation of new coffee shops have sprung up serving everything from espresso, cappuccino and latte to in-house blends. Despite this,

tea is still the most popular non-alcoholic beverage for the Irish. Taken with plenty of milk, and offered by the cup or the mug, it's drunk throughout the day – with meals, or as a thirst quencher during a break from shopping. It's always offered to friends to welcome them on arrival – either on its own, or with biscuits or a few home-made scones.

What to see
Practicalities

## FINDING OUT

Two magazines sold by all newspaper sellers cover most of what's happening in Dublin. *In Dublin* and *Hot Press* (IR£1.95/€2.50) are published every other Wednesday. Besides news reports, interviews and reviews, they contain up-to-date listings of events. *In Dublin* also lists the addresses of clubs and late bars, as well as giving details of live gigs. *The Event Guide,* a free newspaper that's available just about everywhere (and can always be found at the Irish Film Centre in Temple Bar), offers the same type of information. Make sure you get hold of one or the other, if you want to make the most of Dublin's thriving cultural life.

## GETTING ABOUT

As Dublin is a relatively small city and not particularly hilly, the best way to get around is on foot. It's certainly ideal if you want to explore the hidden corners of the city. Another bonus is that the most pleasant shopping districts are pedestrianized – Grafton Street, Henry Street and part of Temple Bar. Forget about bikes, unless you're wearing a helmet and enjoy living dangerously. Irish drivers are anything but calm and controlled, and the driving of the bus drivers can best be described as sporty. Car hire is another alternative you might want to consider, but really only recommended if you're planning to stay on a little longer and visit the surrounding area (see p. 8). Parking is notoriously bad in the city centre and having a car is often a hindrance when you're trying to get around.

## BY BUS AND DART

Two good public transport networks make it easy to get around Dublin. Double-decker buses allow a more elevated view of the city. Timetables are available from the head office of Dublin Bus Company, 59 O'Connell Street Upper ☎ 873 4222 (Mon.-Sat. 8.30am-5.30pm). It's best to buy tickets in advance (see below) as you'll need the right money once you're on the bus and drivers don't give change. Depending on the distance travelled, prices range from 60p/€0.76 to IR£1.30/€1.65. The main stops in the city centre are in O'Connell Street (going north), Abbey Street (north and west), Eden Quay (south) and in the vicinity of Trinity College and St Stephen's Green. Buses that go to the city centre from the outskirts have *An Lár* ('city centre' in Gaelic) on the front. Bus stops are marked by

small signs bearing the words 'Dublin Bus' and showing the number of the line. Buses run from 6am-11.30pm every 10-15 minutes, but the Nitelink service runs on Thursday, Friday and Saturday nights at 1am, 2am and 3am in almost all directions (from a stop near Trinity College, on the corner of College Street and Westmoreland Street, with tickets priced IR£3-4.50/€3.80-5.70 on sale on the buses and from a few shops displaying the Nitelink logo). The DART (Dublin Area Rapid Transit) is a fast suburban train that links the city centre with the shore districts, between Howth in the north and Bray in the south. It runs from 6.30am-11.30pm, every 5 minutes at peak times and every 15 minutes at other times. Tickets (priced 80p-IR£2/€1-2.50) are on sale at the city's four stations,

Connolly Station, Tara Street, Pearse Street and Lansdowne Road. Reduced-rate tickets include the Adult One-Day Rambler Ticket, which allows one day's unlimited travel on buses (IR£3.50/€4.45), the Family Day Bus Ticket, valid for 2 adults and up to 4 children (IR£5.70/€7.25 bus only and IR£7.50/€9.50 bus and DART), and the Dublin Three-Day Rambler (IR£6.50/€8.25 per adult for 3 days on all buses, including Airlink, the airport transfer bus). The Dublin Explorer Ticket allows 4 days' unlimited travel by bus and DART (IR£10/€12.70 per adult).

## BY TAXI

You can pick up a taxi at a taxi rank, generally found close to bus stops and big hotels, with the taxis lined up in order of arrival. O'Connell Street, St Stephen's Green and

College Green are the main thoroughfares. Alternatively, call one from your hotel or B&B. Expect to pay a flat rate of IR£2/€2.50 per person, plus a supplement of 50p/€0.65 per additional passenger or item of luggage. The price (around IR£1.50/€2 a mile) is then shown on the meter .

## BUS AND COACH TOURS

If you want to get an overall picture of the city before concentrating on particular districts, it's a good idea to start with a guided city tour in a double-decker bus. The commentaries are informative and often quite entertaining. All the tours leave from the central office on O'Connell Street and last an hour and a quarter (price IR£7/€9, leaving every hour from 10am). You can buy a ticket for the Dublin City Hop on-Hop off which is valid for the whole day and allows you to get off at each of the thirteen stops to have a look round before continuing on the next bus (IR£8/€10).

Romantics may prefer a tour in a horse-drawn carriage in the Georgian districts around Merrion Square and the Grand Canal. The starting point is the north side of St Stephen's Green, at the end of Grafton Street. The carriage costs IR£20/€25 and seats up to four people. Phoenix Park also offers excursions of this kind.

## THEMED TOURS

If a tour of the city's most famous musical pubs appeals to you, the Musical Pub Crawl leaves every evening from St John Gogarty's (Temple Bar), and takes you from pub to pub in the company of traditional musicians for two and a half hours (May-Oct., every evening 7.30pm, Nov.-Apr., Fri.-Sat. evenings 7.30pm, price IR£6/€7.50). The Literary Pub Crawl, led by actors who perform from the works of Ireland's great writers, leaves The Duke pub (Duke Street) and takes you to Dublin's best-known literary pubs (Easter-Oct., Mon.-Sat. 7.30pm, Sun. noon and 7.30pm, Nov.-Easter, Thu.-Sat. 7.30pm, Sun. noon and 7.30pm, price IR£6.50/€8.25). In the same vein, the Historical Walking Tour follows in the footsteps of the main events and buildings that have marked the history of Dublin (leaving from the portal of Trinity College, May-Sep., Mon.-Fri. 11am and 3pm, Sat.-Sun. 11am, noon and 3pm., Oct.-Apr., Fri.-Sun., noon, price IR£4/€5).

## TELEPHONES AND EMAIL

If you've got a mobile phone, check that your contract is valid overseas Dublin and Ireland are fully covered by the networks. Phoning from your hotel room or B&B will cost up to 30% more than it should. There are plenty of *Eircom* and *Esat* phone boxes that take coins or phone cards (on sale at newsagents').

A very cheap, practical solution if you want to phone home is the prepaid *torc* card that comes with a code allowing you to use it to make calls from your hotel room, a phone box or any other fixed phone. You can buy it at the International Call Shop, 46 Temple Bar, every day 10am-11pm. To call abroad, dial 00 followed by the code of the country in question (44 for Great Britain, 1 for the USA and Canada, 61 for Australia and 64 for New Zealand) followed by the number of the person you're calling (minus the initial 0).

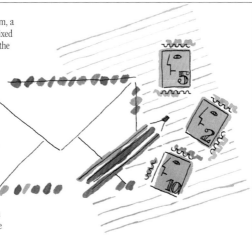

To pick up or send emails, try the Global Internet Café, 8 O'Connell Street Lower, which is open every day 9am-11pm.

## SENDING POSTCARDS AND LETTERS

Letterboxes, which are green, can be found all over the the city. Stamps are sold in post offices (O'Connell Street,

Anne Street South and St Andrew Street) and some newsagents. The General Post Office (GPO), in O'Connell Street, is open every day. (weekdays, 8am-8pm, Sun. 10.30am-6pm). Mail takes 3-5 days to reach continental Europe, and a stamp for a letter or postcard costs 30p/€0.38.

## CHANGING MONEY

You'll need cash for pubs and small purchases, but all the shops, hotels and most B&Bs take credit cards (Visa and Mastercard). You can change your money before you go but, as you're only here for a weekend, it's probably best to get local currency from a cash machine. A commission is charged every time you take out money, so get all you need in one go. There are several cash machines at the airport and there are plenty in the city centre. The bureaux de change in the General Post Office and in Westmoreland

Street are open on Sundays for changing travellers' cheques. Don't forget that Ireland is in the Euro Zone, and that the pound ceases to be legal tender from 9 February 2002. From then the Irish currency will be the euro, although you'll still be able to change pound notes in banks for a while (see also p. 8).

## OPENING TIMES

The banks are open Mon.-Fri., 10am-4pm, Thu. 10am-5pm. Pubs are open Mon.-Wed. 10.30am-11.30pm, Thu.-Sat. 10.30am-12.30am and Sun. 12.30-11.30pm. The museums are closed on Sunday mornings and Mondays, and are usually open 10am-5pm. Two chemist's shops stay open late most nights in the city centre – O'Connell's Late Night Pharmacies, 55 O'Connell Street Lower (open Mon.-Sat. 7.30am-10pm, Sun. 10am-10pm) and 21 Grafton Street (open Mon.-Sat 8.30am-8.30pm, Sun. 11am-6pm).

# O'Connell Street, hotbed of Irish resistance

Dublin Writers Museum ⑭
⑫ ⑬
Hugh Lane Gallery of Modern Art
⑪
Rotunda Hospital and Gate Theatre ⑩

St Mary's Pro Cathedral ⑨

Moore Street Market
⑤ ⑧ ⑥ ⑦
Henry St.
General Post Office ③ ④
② Abbey St. Lower
Abbey St. Mid.
Bachelors Walk
Eden Quay
① River Liffey

O'Connell Street, north of the River Liffey, was once the finest avenue in the capital. Despite the fast-food restaurants and souvenir shops, it still has a certain grandeur. A centre of Irish resistance, it was once the scene of bloody events whose history can be traced in its monuments. Now the cinema and theatre district, it's also the site of a picturesque daily market.

for every occasion, from St Valentine's Day to Halloween to birthdays.

### ① O'Connell Bridge★
This very wide bridge built in the late 18th century is the main thoroughfare of the city. It provides a view of the famous Half Penny Bridge upstream, and the imposing Custom House and docks downstream. To the south lies the Trinity College district, and to the north O'Connell Street, with its central tree-lined walk.

### ② Eason's★
80 Abbey Street Middle
☎ 873 3811
Mon.-Wed., Sat. 8.30am-6.45pm, Thu. 8.30am-8.45pm, Fri. 8.30am-7.45pm.

A vast bookshop and newsagent's where you can find fine books, guidebooks in several languages and, on the first floor, a wide choice of maps and gifts, including cuddly toys and knick-knacks

### ③ General Post Office★★
Corner of O'Connell Street and Henry Street
Mon.-Sat. 8am-8pm, Sun. 10.30am-6.30pm.
Entry free.

With its enormous columns, Dublin's post office looks more like a temple than a municipal building. Built in the 19th century, it was stormed in 1916 by the Irish rebels during the Easter

Rising. For six days they made it their headquarters, until they were finally dislodged by the British army. The paintings inside tell the tale, and a statue of the dying Cuchulainn commemorates the rebels who lost their lives here.

#### ❹ Big Jim Larkin★

The statue with raised arms which stands in front of Clery's department store is that of James Larkin, one

of the foremost Irish trade union leaders. In 1913 he urged on the strikers who paralysed the city for over six months from the balcony of the shop with the words, 'The great appear greater because we are on our

---

### A BAWDY SENSE OF HUMOUR

The Dubliners have a bawdy sense of humour that combines with their love of word play in the nicknames they give to the city's statues. Anna Livia is called 'the floozie in the jacuzzi' or 'the hoor (whore) in the sewer', while the statue of Joyce, despite the high esteem in which the writer is held, is commonly known as 'the prick with the stick'.

---

knees. Let us rise.' The strike ended in bloodshed when it was crushed by the police and many protestors were injured.

#### ❺ Moore Street Market★★

This colourful market, which is held every morning, involves an amazing jumble of stalls and activity, including horse carts, fishmongers, fruit and vegetable sellers and pound stalls – and you may even find people selling illicit cigarettes and tobacco. This corner of the city has

so far escaped the economic boom of the so-called 'Celtic Tiger'.

#### ❻ James Joyce★

The nonchalant-looking gentleman leaning on his cane on the corner of O'Connell Street and Earl Street North is in fact a statue of Dublin's most famous son, James Joyce (see box opposite). The *enfant terrible* of Irish literature broke all the accepted rules of English writing and, perhaps inevitably, soon fell foul of the censor.

#### ❼ Madigan's★
**25 Earl Street North**
☎ **874 0646.**

One of Dublin's many pubs, Madigan's has a long bar

room
decked out in
traditional
wooden panelling and old
mirrors. You can have lunch
here for under IR£7 (€9)
and in summer you can have
an inexpensive dinner from
5-10pm. It's the ideal place
for a quiet chat. Don't expect
loud music; the locals come
here to socialize.

### 8 Anna Livia★

Shaded by trees, the strange
statue of the proud, if
somewhat stiff, woman lying

in a fountain was erected in
1988 to celebrate the city's
millennium. The design was
meant to embody the spirit of
the River Liffey, as in Joyce's
*Finnegan's Wake.* However,
instead of impressing and
inspiring Dubliners, Anna
has unfortunately become
the butt of dirty jokes.

### 9 St Mary's Pro Cathedral★
Open every day 8am-7pm.
Entry free.

Set apart from O'Connell
Street, the 19th-century
Catholic cathedral resembles
a Greek temple. Initially
planned for the main avenue,
it was built instead on this
modest street in order not to
provoke the Protestants. 'Pro'
in this case is an abbreviation
of 'provisional'. The Catholics
hoped one day to
recover the great Protestant
St Patrick's cathedral, but it
never happened.

### 10 Rotunda Hospital and Gate Theatre★
Parnell Square
☎ 874 4045
Booking office open
10am-7pm.

At the top of O'Connell Street,
the façade with a pediment
surmounted by a pinnacle
turret belongs to the world's
first maternity hospital,
founded in 1752. The proud
architecture is a reminder
that this was once the
smartest district in the city.
Part of it has been turned
into a cinema, while the rest
houses the Gate Theatre,
venue for the city's most
significant artistic creations
since the 1980s.

### 11 Garden of Remembrance★
Parnell Square North
Open dawn-dusk.
Entry free.

By the time you get here, you
should have realized the
importance in Ireland of the
fight for freedom. This
garden, located on the very
spot where the 1916 rebels
were held, is dedicated to
the memory of all who gave
their lives for Irish

independence. The impressive bronze statue, the *Children of Lir*, dates from 1966 and was the work of Oisín Kelly.

EVERYDAY SHOPPING

If you want to discover a noisily authentic Dublin, far from Internet start-ups and the new economy, take a walk down Earl Street North or Henry Street, where kitsch stalls stand side by side with bazaars and cheap clothes stores. On Saturdays the streets are packed with families enjoying their weekly outing, a reminder of the pre-boom city of Roddy Doyle's novels.

It represents four children who were turned into swans by their wicked stepmother, a reference to an ancient Irish legend and a poem by Yeats.

### ⓬ Dublin Writers Museum★★

18 Parnell Square North
☎ 872 2077
Open Sep.-May, Mon.-Sat. 10am-5pm, Sun. 11am-5pm. Jun.-Aug., Mon.-Fri. 10am-6pm, Sat.-Sun. 11am-5pm. Entry charge.

This museum introduces visitors to Ireland many famous writers by means of documents, personal belongings and portraits. If you've only heard of Joyce and Wilde, this is a good way of familiarizing yourself with the others, but it's a pity living authors are left out. Don't miss the bookshop, and have a piece of cake or light lunch in the tearoom overlooking the fine Zen garden.

### ⓭ Hugh Lane Gallery of Modern Art★★

Parnell Square North
☎ 874 1903
Open Tue.-Thu. 9.30am-6pm, Fri.-Sat. 9.30am-5pm, Sun. 11am-5pm. Entry free, but IR£6 (€7.50) charge for Francis Bacon studio.

Housed in a fine Georgian residence, this museum displays works by 19th and 20th-century Irish and European artists, such as Jack Yeats, Roderick O'Conor, Manet, Monet, Degas, Christo and Francis Bacon. Recently renovated, the house has marvellous interior architecture, a domed ceiling, many stained-glass windows and a magnificent stairwell.

### ⓮ The James Joyce Centre★

35 North Great Georges Street
☎ 878 8547
Open Mon.-Sat. 9.30am-5pm, Sun. 12.30-4.30pm. Entry charge.

If you admire both the author James Joyce and Georgian Dublin, you should love this museum and information centre, which aims to shed light on the writer's work in any way that it can. The guided tour is conducted by his affable nephew, and is accompanied by an interesting video which concentrates on early 20th-century Dublin.

# From Custom House to the Bank of Ireland

Dublin's wealth once relied on the trade from its thriving port. From Custom House take an invigorating walk towards the docks, which no longer hum with activity, but still smell of the sea. Not far away stands one of the city's most famous theatres, as well as a series of warm, welcoming pubs frequented by actors and journalists.

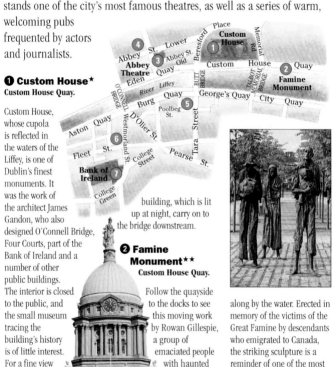

## ❶ Custom House★
**Custom House Quay.**

Custom House, whose cupola is reflected in the waters of the Liffey, is one of Dublin's finest monuments. It was the work of the architect James Gandon, who also designed O'Connell Bridge, Four Courts, part of the Bank of Ireland and a number of other public buildings. The interior is closed to the public, and the small museum tracing the building's history is of little interest. For a fine view of the whole building, which is lit up at night, carry on to the bridge downstream.

## ❷ Famine Monument★★
**Custom House Quay.**

Follow the quayside to the docks to see this moving work by Rowan Gillespie, a group of emaciated people with haunted faces staggering

along by the water. Erected in memory of the victims of the Great Famine by descendants who emigrated to Canada, the striking sculpture is a reminder of one of the most terrible periods in Ireland's history, when over 1,000,000 people died of starvation and around 1,500,000 others were forced to emigrate.

## ❸ Abbey Theatre★
**Abbey Street Lower**
☎ **878 7222.**

A century ago, Irish poet W.B. Yeats and his friends Lady Gregory and the writer J.M. Synge, founded this institution with the purpose

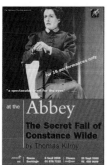

of putting on innovative plays. Performances were often jeered by the audience. Though the present building (the old one was destroyed by fire) is disappointing, the theatre remains an important centre of literary and theatrical creation. Today the great classics are performed alongside the works of young contemporary writers.

and a chat. On Thursday evenings, drinkers cram into the basement to listen to live music.

### ❺ Mulligan's★★
**8 Poolbeg Street**
**☎ 677 5582.**

Another day, another pub, this time the haunt of the journalists who work nearby. Dating back to 1782, it has acquired a certain patina, and is often a place of lively debate among regulars. The Guinness here is said to be the best in the city. Joyce often frequented Mulligan's, as did J.F. Kennedy, who stayed for a time in Dublin writing for American newspapers, just after the Second World War.

### ❻ PALACE BAR★★
**21 Fleet Street**
**☎ 677 9290.**

You may become quite blasé about the pubs in Dublin after a while, but a visit to the Palace is a whole new experience. Once frequented by poets and playwrights, it's a charming, old-fashioned place in the banking and university district. You can drink a delicious pint here (among the least expensive in the city) in a quiet atmosphere that leaves the hustle and bustle of the city far behind. It's definitely a must if you're on a pub crawl.

### ❹ The Flowing Tide★★
**9 Abbey Street Lower**
**☎ 874 4106.**

The decor of this pub, much frequented by actors after rehearsals and performances, has remained unchanged for years, with stained-glass windows and panelled walls covered in portraits of artistes. In the daytime it's a quiet place to enjoy a break

### ❼ Bank of Ireland★★
**2 College Green**
**☎ 677 6801**
**Open Mon.-Fri. 10am-4pm,**
**Thu. 10am-5pm.**
**Entry free.**

This building with its pompous columns was originally the seat of the Irish Parliament. Built in 1729, it ceased to perform this function when the parliament was dissolved in

order to join the British Parliament in London. The Bank of Ireland later acquired the building for £40,000 and preserved the chamber of the House of Lords, with its gigantic table and rich panelling, intact. The House of Commons, complete with its dome, is now used as the banking hall.

# A romantic walk along the Liffey

A legendary river lined with fine hotels, the Liffey flows effortlessly through the city. Long abandoned, the quayside has begun to come back to life, with art galleries and restaurants opening along its length. No one should spend time in Dublin without crossing the romantic Ha'penny Bridge and trying some oysters in one of the bars.

### ❶ Ha'penny Bridge★★

The most popular view of Dublin – an attractive metal footbridge spanning the Liffey which leads into the trendy

district of Temple Bar. With a silhouette that appears quite insubstantial in the half-light, and old-fashioned street lamps, it dates from 1816 and owes its name to the toll demanded until 1919 to cross it. Upstream is the Millennium Bridge, a footbridge built for the year 2000. The impressive dome of Four Courts acts as a backdrop.

### ❷ The Winding Stairs★

**40 Ormond Quay Lower**
☎ 873 3292
**Open Mon.-Sat. 9.30am-6pm (Thu. & Fri. open until 8pm), Sun. 1-6pm.**

A tiny bookshop of nooks and crannies, lined with second-hand books on two floors – old editions of the Irish classics, illustrated books on Ireland, texts in Gaelic and beautiful maps. On the third floor is a coffee shop where you can have tea and cake or a light lunch as you watch the Liffey flow by.

### ❹ Music Hall of Fame★★★

**57 Abbey Street Middle**
☎ 878 3345
**Open every day 10.30am-5.30pm. Entry charge.**

A lively, interactive museum that takes visitors through the story of Irish music, with a reconstruction of an old country pub, a high-quality soundtrack and featuring a

### **3** THE HAGS WITH THE BAGS★

The two women who sit comfortably, deep in conversation on a bench at the side of Liffey Street are surprisingly realistic. Officially called *Meeting Place*, the work naturally soon acquired a humorous nickname and Dubliners kept up their time-honoured tradition of word-play by naming it 'the hags with the bags'.

range of musical styles – from the country dance music of the 1950s to the frantic rock of U2 and the Undertones. It's a fascinating measure of the incredible diversity and creativity of Irish musicians.

### **5** Irish Historical Pictures★
5 Ormond Quay Lower
☎ 872 0144
Open Mon.-Fri. 8am-6pm,
Sat.-Sun. 8am-5pm.

This collection of 16,000 originals, including scenes and landscapes from all over Ireland, is a goldmine for collectors of reproductions, engravings and old photographs. Prints can be mounted up with a matching border (from IR£12/€15 according to size) and taken away or posted to your home address.

### **6** Bridge Art Gallery★★
6 Ormond Quay Upper
☎ 872 9702
Open Mon.-Sat. 10am-6pm,
Sun. 2-5pm.

Sculptures and paintings by young contemporary Irish artists, including exuberant statues by Lucy Morrow, ceramic 'flat faces' by Christy Keeney, photographs by Janet Preston, and reproductions by Noelle Noonan.

### **7** Four Courts★
Inns Quay.

Built by the same architect as the Custom House, Four Courts, the capital's law courts, was completed in 1802. In 1923 it was the scene

of violent confrontations between the opponents of the treaty conceding Northern Ireland to England, who were occupying the building, and the troops of Michael Collins, who had negotiated the said agreement, who were posted on the other bank of the Liffey. The building and archives were destroyed, but an identical version was built in 1932.

### **8** St Michan's Church★
Church Street
☎ 872 4154
Open 15 Mar.-31 Oct.
10am-12.45pm, 2-4.45pm,
Nov.-mid-Mar. 12.30-3.30pm.
Closed Sat. pm and Sun.
Entry charge.

The rather uninteresting exterior of this church gives no clue about its amazing occupants. The bodies housed in the crypt have been mummified by the dry atmosphere and constant temperature, and have been preserved almost intact. The wooden coffins have split open due to the conditions and the bodies, complete with skin and hair, are clearly visible. The oldest is thought to date from the time of the Crusades, in the 13th century. There's also an organ that was played by Handel with some fine woodcarving.

# The Trinity College district

From the warm panelling of the great university library with its Celtic treasures, to the fine shops of Nassau Street, this is a varied and appealing district. Look in the shops for traditional crafts, high-quality tweeds, cosy knitwear, rustic pottery and elegant crystal, alongside the minimalist creations of the new designers.

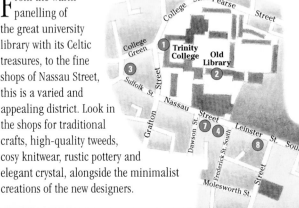

### ❶ Trinity College★
Entry free.

The oldest university in Ireland was founded in 1592 by Elizabeth I of England. Reserved for Protestants until 1873, it was a potent symbol of English domination. The most famous Irish writers, including Jonathan Swift, Synge and Oscar Wilde, studied here. Once you pass through the imposing gateway, the old-fashioned campus seems a world away from the hustle and bustle of the street. On the left is the chapel where the students perform mass. The red brick buildings are the oldest.

### ❷ Old Library and Book of Kells★★★
Trinity College
☎ 608 1171
Open Oct.-May, Mon.-Sat. 9.30am-4.30pm, Jun.-Sep., Sun. noon-4.30pm, 9.30am-4.30pm. Entry charge.

The library of Trinity College is housed in a vast room 65m/215ft long and 15m/50ft high. Around 200,000 old books are stacked under the panelled vault, including sacred medieval manuscripts, such as the Book of Kells (the best known), the Book of Armagh and the Book of Durrow. The illuminations and calligraphy make them world treasures. The harp, the symbol of Ireland, dates from the Middle Ages.

### ❸ O'Neill's★
2 Suffolk Street
☎ 679 3671.

This popular pub is the place where the world of finance meets the student body. In Viking times, this was a raised area that served as an assembly place. The pub has five separate bars inside. Noisy and often packed, it reflects the dynamism of the city.

### ❹ Blarney Woollen Mills★

**21-23 Nassau Street**
**☎ 671 0068**
**Open Mon.-Sat. 9am-6pm,**
**Thu. 9am-8pm,**
**Sun. 11am-6pm.**

One of the more traditional shops in the street selling a selection of high-quality craft products at reasonable prices, including hand-knitted Aran sweaters, table linen and lace, wool and mohair plaids, caps and scarves.

### ❺ National Museum★★★

**Kildare Street**
**☎ 677 7444**
**Open Tue.-Sat. 10am-5pm,**
**Sun. 2-5pm.**
**Entry free.**

### ❼ EASONS HANNA BOOKSHOP AND CAFÉ★

**Corner of Nassau Street**
**and Dawson Street**
**☎ 677 1255.**

The mezzanine of this bookshop houses a small traditional tearoom offering fresh scones, cream cakes and light snacks overlooking the book-covered tables. Here you'll find lots of students, reasonable prices and a relaxed atmosphere.

This museum offers a glimpse of prehistoric Ireland, with incredible Bronze Age artefacts and fabulous gold jewellery, some of which dates from the 8th century BC. Particularly interesting are the curiously ornate necklaces and the famous Tara Brooch (8th century) that's copied in all the shops.

### ❻ Leinster House★

**Kildare Street**
**☎ 618 3000**
**Visits by appointment to**
**attend the sessions.**
**Entry free.**

The imposing building occupying the far side of the courtyard between the National Museum and the National Library has been the venue for the debates of the National Parliament (House of Representatives and Senate) since 1922. It was originally the grandiose residence of the Duke of Leinster and is said to have inspired the architect of the White House in Washington. The rear façade overlooking Merrion Square is the most impressive, with vast lawns. The whole ensemble typifies the Georgian period in all its elegance.

### ❽ Kilkenny Centre★★

**5-6 Nassau Street**
**☎ 677 7066**
**Open Mon.-Fri. 8.30am-**
**6.30pm (Thu. open until**
**8pm), Sat. 9am-6pm,**
**Sun. 11am-6pm.**

A smart 'department store' which showcases the work of craftsmen and designers, from sophisticated linen knitwear and dresses and jackets by Louise Kennedy, to the refined, elegant clothes of Kilkenny's own label. What about splashing out on a piece of pottery by Stephen Pearce or Michael Kennedy, or a soft tartan blanket in bright colours?

# Around Grafton Street, the shopping mecca

Between Trinity College and St Stephen's Green lies the shopping centre of the capital. All the finest shops are here, in a network of picturesque alleyways and passages. Take time for a tea or coffee break under the glass roof of Bewley's or in a confectioner's as you explore this shopper's paradise. A number of shops are open on Sunday afternoons – a definite plus.

Dame Street
3
Dame Lane
Dame St.
Georges St. Great
Exchequer Street
St. Andrew St.
Suffolk St.
Nassau Street
1
Wicklow Street
2
11
Castle Market
South Street
Powerscourt Townhouse Centre
8
9
Johnson Court
10
12
Drury Street
William Street
Westbury Mall
7
Duke Street
4
5
6
Dawson Street
13
20
14
Harry St.
Clarendon Street
15
Grafton Street
16
Anne Street South
17
18
St Ann's Church
Chatham St.
19
King Street South

## ❷ Butler's Chocolate Café★★
24 Wicklow Street
☎ 671 0591
Open Mon.-Tue.
8am-6pm, Wed.,
Fri.-Sat. 8am-7pm,
Thu. 8am-9pm, Sun.
11am-6pm.

## ❶ The International★★★
23 Wicklow Street
☎ 677 9250.

A great bar, dating from the late 18th century, with multi-coloured windows that shed golden light on the velour banquettes and magnificently carved mahogany panelling behind the vast marble bar. The atmosphere is amazing, with music in the evening at weekends. From 12.30pm on Sundays, a session by visiting musicians or regulars will wake you up a treat.

Delicious coffee in all its forms to drink with the chocolates sold individually in the shop. Afterwards you can have a box of your choice made up (IR£4-12/€5-15 according to weight). An in-place to eat that makes a change from the usual tea and scones.

## MOLLY MALONE

Right at the entrance to Grafton Street, coming from Trinity College, the statue of a buxom young street-seller depicts Molly Malone, made famous by the song. She symbolises the city, but is also a reminder of the desperate poverty of a people reduced to begging for pennies in the streets. The curved form and generous bosom of the statue scarcely reflect the sad reality. Dubliners immediately dubbed her 'the tart with the cart', and many even slip money between her breasts.

## ❸ Stag's Head★★
**1 Dame Court**
☎ 679 3701.

This pub has preserved its original Victorian decor intact, with a bar of red Connemara marble, plenty

of well-aged wooden panelling and a warm, lively atmosphere, all bathed in a dim half-light. Come here to sample some of the best pub food in Dublin, served 12.30-3.30pm, including dishes such as traditional bacon and cabbage. You'll always find a warm welcome, too.

## ❹ Marks & Spencer★
**15-20 Grafton Street**
☎ 679 7855
**Open Mon.-Sat. 9am-7pm, Thu. 9am-9pm, Sun. noon-6pm.**

Even if you don't come for the shopping, which is pretty conventional, come for the well-preserved interior architecture, which gives you a feel of the English shops of the Victorian era, with their vast, brightly-lit spaces and wide, majestic staircases. The premises were originally

occupied by Brown Thomas, which has unfortunately given in to the call of modernity and moved across the way.

## ❺ The Duke★★
**9 Duke Street**
☎ 679 9553.

The finest of the literary pubs has walls decorated with drawings, loads of nooks and crannies in which to meet friends, and a traditional

decor. It's packed by late afternoon, with a wide variety of people, from university lecturers to businessmen to journalists, all talking nineteen to the dozen.

## ❻ Apollo Gallery★★
**51c Dawson Street**
☎ 671 2609
**Open Mon.-Sat. 10.30am-6pm, Thu. 10.30am-8pm, Sun. noon-6pm.**

A wide variety of contemporary Irish artists are regularly displayed here, particularly

the painters Graham Knuttel (who produces large, brightly-coloured oil paintings and interesting sculptures, too), George Dunne, Marie Carroll and Markey Robinson. Other works range from simple watercolours portraying melancholic landscapes, to large, exuberant canvases executed in bold brushstrokes.

### ❼ Westbury Mall★

This lovely old-fashioned shopping arcade opening on to Johnson Court, an alleyway that itself opens on

to Grafton Street, houses some fine interior decoration and gift shops, as well as a tearoom. On the right are Clarendon Street and Powerscourt, while Harry Street is opposite.

### ❽ Powerscourt Townhouse Centre★★

**Clarendon Street and William Street South**
**Open Mon.-Sat. 10am-6pm,**
**Thu. 10am-8pm,**
**Sun. noon-6pm.**

Once the townhouse belonging to an 18th-century lord, this is now a very smart shopping centre. The William

Street façade is the most impressive. Lord Powerscourt was nicknamed 'the French count', as he always dressed in the latest Paris fashions. The enormous structure is built around a central patio with restaurants and coffee shops. All around on the mezzanine is a succession of beautiful shops and galleries, selling jewellery, antiques and luxury ready-to-wear clothing. Don't miss the Design Centre on the top floor and the finest creations of the best young Irish designers.

### ❾ Gloria Jean's Coffees★

**Powerscourt Townhouse Centre**
☎ 679 7772
**Open Mon.-Sat. 8am-8pm,**
**Thu. 8am-8pm,**
**Sun. 10am-7pm.**

With fifteen kinds of hot and chilled coffee on offer, this is the ideal place to take a break. You can also buy one of the shop's thirty-four varieties of ground coffee, as well as original coffeepots, teapots and cups. Big-cat prints and animal shapes seem to be popular.

### ⑩ La Maison des Gourmets★★
**15 Castle Market**
☎ **672 7258**
**Open Mon.-Sat. 9am-6pm (Thu. 9am-7pm).**

A place to make for if you're tired of fruit cake. A French master pastry cook prepares the most delicious light gateaux and a variety of canapés, main courses and salads to take away. Choose between the small terrace and the tiny elegant tearoom on the first floor.

### ⑪ Market Arcade★
This little arcade between Castle Market and South Great George's Street resembles a flea market, with its second-hand clothes dealers, second-hand booksellers, costume jewellery sellers, and the wafts of incense coming from the shops. You'll find cheap snacks here, and gourmet food stalls as well.

### ⑫ The Long Hall★★
**51 South Great Georges Street**
☎ **475 1590.**

Another atmospheric pub where time seems to have stood still amid the chandeliers, mirrors and woodwork. A long bar room with comfortable seats, in the warm glow of stained-glass windows and a hushed silence to relax in after a day of shopping. Nothing appears to have changed here since the day it opened, in 1880.

### ⑬ Bewley's★★
**6 Grafton Street**
☎ **677 6761**
**Open every day 7.30am-11pm.**

This huge tearoom on two floors has been a Dublin institution since 1842. You can eat here cheaply at any time of day in an old-Dublin setting of mahogany and stained-glass windows, though the main area is now unfortunately self-service. The mezzanine is more pleasant, where you're served by traditionally-dressed waitresses. Readings and

concerts are held regularly in the café theatre in the Oriental Room.

## THE IRISH COVENT GARDEN

Grafton Street isn't just a fine shopping district, it's also one of the Dubliners' favourite places for a weekend stroll. People come here to look round the shops and watch the street artists, who are present in large numbers when it isn't raining. Mime artists, portraitists, musicians and contorsionists all delight the passers-by. The Irish make a good audience, marvelling at everything and making colourful comments, which only adds to the atmosphere.

### ⓴ Bruxelles★
**7 Harry Street**
☎ 677 5362
**(Live music on occasional evenings).**

The most noticeable thing about this pub, built in 1890, is its fine neo-Gothic façade and turrets. The inside is equally interesting, and at peak times it's one of the in places to meet, with a young,

densely packed crowd that overflows on to the pavement. The terrace, with its view of the stream of passers-by emerging from nearby Grafton Street, is pleasant on fine days. At least twice a week, and more in season, you'll find light music being played. There's always plenty of atmosphere.

### ⓯ McDaid's★
**3 Harry Street**
☎ 679 4395.

A legendary pub, well known to fans of Irish literature. The greatest writers used to meet here regularly, especially three who were renowned for their drinking abilities – Patrick Kavanagh, Brendan Behan and Flann O'Brien. Many others followed in their footsteps in the 1950s, making the pub a nerve centre of literary creation. Nowadays the atmosphere is young and trendy and there are jazz concerts on Sunday evenings, and sometimes on Wednesdays as well.

### ⓰ John Kehoe's★★
**9 Anne Street South**
☎ 677 8312.

Easily a favourite among Dublin pubs, with its original floor and cosy booths separated by wooden partitions that make a pleasant place for a friendly chat. It's quiet in the daytime, which makes it the ideal setting for the sort of interminable philosophical

conversations that are traditional in the capital, but by late afternoon, it gets packed and it's standing room only.

### ⓱ Sheridan★★
**11 Anne Street South**
☎ 679 3143
**Open Mon.-Sat. 9am-6pm.**

Ireland is definitely a land proud of its cheeses. For proof of this, pop along to this tiny shop imbued with the smell of fresh milk and the countryside. There are numerous cheeses made from cow's milk, which change according to the season (try the Cashel Blue), a few small goat's milk cheeses (such as Mine Gabhar), and ewe's milk cheese from the Cratloe Hills.

### ⓲ St Ann's Church★
**Dawson Street**
**Open Mon.-Fri. 10am-4pm.**

The neo-Romanesque architecture of this Anglican church dating from 1707 is fairly bland, but there's a rather nice touch inside. On a shelf to the left of the altar,

The brick façade is easily identified by the distinctive lamps that are held in supports in the shape of arms. The atmosphere inside is warm and hushed, with mahogany, marble and shiny brass.

### ⑳ The Hat Studio★
**33 Clarendon Street**
☎ **679 7988**
**Open Mon.-Sat. 10.30am-6pm, Thu. noon-7.30pm.**

You can buy the most amazing hats in Dublin here – from little headpieces to more extravagant examples – in every conceivable colour. Fashionable women come

you'll see one or two stale loaves left for the poor in accordance with charitable tradition. It's customary for

120 loaves to be left here each week and for anyone to be able to help themselves without being asked any questions. There are free lunchtime concerts on some days (details in entrance).

## PUB CRAWLS

Dublin's countless pubs are undoubtedly a major feature of the city, and pub crawls are nothing less than a national sport. You will have to plan your route carefully to take in one or more districts, and never drink enough to lose your sense of direction. If you need a pretext, then why not take a tour of the literary pubs? Or, failing that, the musical ones, or those with the finest decors? There's no limit to the choice available – those listed here are simply the most inviting.

### ⑲ Chatham Lounge★
**1 Chatham Street**
☎ **677 8596.**

Also known as Neary's, this is the meeting place for the people from the nearby Gaiety Theatre (the back door leads to the wings). In the evening a cosmopolitan crowd, and the actors who come here after the performance, guarantee an interesting atmosphere.

here to order their hats for the horse-racing season. The spring and summer collections are irresistible from March onwards.

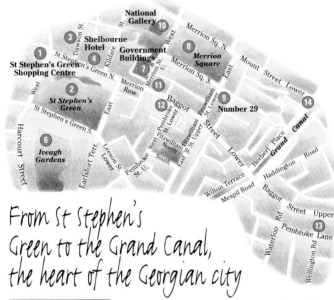

## From St Stephen's Green to the Grand Canal, the heart of the Georgian city

Departing from Dublin's most popular park, this tour takes you around the Georgian city, where the streets are lined with fine brick houses. This smart residential district of the capital is also known as 'Dublin 4', because of its postcode. Here you'll find the seat of government, a number of museums, and pubs where politicians meet. Some of the avenues are so quiet and shady you could almost be in the country.

### ❶ St Stephen's Green Shopping Centre★

**St Stephen's Green West**
**Open Mon.-Wed., Sat. 9am-6pm, Thu.-Fri. 9am-8pm.**

This shopping centre's amazing architecture is reminiscent of the huge structures built in England by the Victorians. Under a vast glass roof, there are two floors of shops of every kind, from cut-price luxury designer clothes and New Age gadgets,

to trendy ready-to-wear. Take a break in the cafeteria overlooking the nearby park.

### ❸ Perk★
**51b Dawson Street (C3)**
**☎ 6720218**
**Open Mon.-Fri. 7.30am-6pm, Sat. 9.30am-6pm.**

This small, contemporary coffee house lives up to its aim of doing simple things well. There's a range of freshly made soups, sandwiches, wraps and confectionery at reasonable prices (sandwiches start at IR£2.65/€3.35). Service is cheerful and friendly. It gets quite busy at lunchtime, but is a perfect spot

for 'elevenses' or an afternoon break. Don't miss their own blend Arabica coffee.

### ❹ Shelbourne Hotel★★
**27 St Stephen's Green North**
**☎ 676 6471.**

This grand hotel dating from 1824 is a symbol of Dublin's British past. Behind its revolving doors lies a different world. Even if you can't afford to stay here, take a peek at the Horseshoe Bar, which has the

atmosphere of an English club. More politicking is done here than in the nearby Parliament. Alternatively, treat yourself to afternoon tea in the Lord Mayor's Lounge (IR£15/€19). Served from 3 to 5.30pm, it's the quintessential British tea, with cakes, small, elegant sandwiches, scones and cream, and a range of teas served in an elegant old-fashioned setting.

### ❺ Newman House★★
**St Stephen's Green South**
**☎ 706 7422**
**Open Jun.-Sep. Tue.-Fri. noon-4pm, Sat. 2-4pm, Sun. 11am-1pm, by appointment the rest of the year. Entry charge.**

In the 19th century these two houses were home to the Catholic university (where James Joyce studied), the counterpart of the Protestant Trinity College. The construction is high Georgian, and the interior decoration is splendid. The

### ❷ St Stephen's Green★★

These 9 hectares/22 acres of natural beauty in the heart of the city attract Dubliners of every kind. At lunchtime, it's peopled by girls in school uniform, businessmen in their shirt-sleeves eating sandwiches, rows of pensioners sitting on benches, and clusters of children feeding the pigeons. The old-fashioned pavilion near the ornamental lake is a haven for courting couples.

walls and ceilings are adorned with highly elaborate Baroque stucco work, including nude figures. Before turning one of the drawing rooms into a chapel, the bishop insisted on having them dressed.

### **6** Iveagh Gardens★

St Stephen's Green is often crowded, but this garden hemmed in by buildings is an unexpectedly peaceful oasis close to the city centre. It has vast lawns, a tinkling fountain, ancient horse chestnut trees and clumps of holly, with old garden walls all around. On the north side there's a sort of open-air theatre, the venue for some highly original performances.

### **7** Government Buildings★
**Merrion Street Upper.**

This imposing building, surrounded by high railings, housed the Royal College of Science in the early 20th century. It's now the seat of a number of ministries, and the *Taoiseach,* or Prime Minister, has his office here. Referring to the high cost of renovating the building, a detractor rechristened it the 'Chas Mahal' ('Chas' as in Charles, the first name of the then Prime Minister).

### **8** Merrion Square★★

This vast Georgian square is typical of late 19th-century Dublin, with its tall brick houses, brightly coloured doors, and wrought-iron gates. Many famous people, including Yeats and Oscar Wilde, have lived in the district. The statue of the latter, made of 40 different kinds of stone, is the curiosity of the park. Sprawled on a rock, he gazes across at the family house opposite with a sarcastic smile on his lips. Some of his most famous aphorisms are engraved on two columns. He, too, has been given a pithy nickname – 'the fag on the crag'.

### **9** Number 29★
**29 Fitzwilliam Street Lower**
☎ **702 6165**
**Open Tue.-Sat. 10am-5pm, Sun. 2-5pm.**
**Entry charge.**

After demolishing twenty or so Georgian houses to build its head office, the ESB (Electricity Supply Board) tried to make up for it by restoring this 18th-century townhouse. The guided tour takes you to the kitchen and the housekeeper's room in the basement, the reception rooms on the ground floor and first floor, the master bedroom and boudoir on the second floor, and the nursery on the top floor, where you can admire the enormous, child-sized doll's house.

### **10** National Gallery★★★
**Merrion Square West**
☎ **661 5133**
**Open Mon.-Sat. 9.30am-5.30pm, Thu. 9.30am-8.30pm, Sun. noon-5.30pm.**
**Entry free.**

Besides a fine selection of works of the Pont-Aven school (including pieces by Paul Henry and Roderick O'Connor), English landscape painters and French artists such as Signac and Van Dongen, the museum owns some marvellous Italian primitives. The room devoted to the Yeats

## ⑭ GRAND CANAL WALK★★

The canal, was dug in the late 18th century to link the west coast to Dublin via the River Shannon, and was at that time the longest in the UK. It hasn't been used for river trade for 40 years, but now provides one of the most pleasant walks in the city, especially between Mount Street and Leeson Street. With its grassy embankments, amateur painters, fishermen and rows of Georgian houses, it has been designated a conservation area. The realistic-looking statue of a man on a bench beside the bank depicts the writer Patrick Kavanagh, who used to come here to write poetry.

family, which features some of its lesser-known members, is also worth seeing. W.B. Yeats's father, brother and sisters, and daughter all made contributions to the collection. Jack Yeats's painting *The Liffey Swim* depicts an existing Dublin tradition that takes place every September – a swimming race in the waters of the Liffey.

## ⑪ Doheny & Nesbitt's★★
**5 Baggot Street Lower**
☎ 676 2945.

This old pub, a haunt of lawyers and politicians, has preserved its wooden partitions and mahogany bar intact. Regulars engage in interminable discussions about the legal and political questions of the day undisturbed by the soft, filtered lighting. Come here to study the art of conversing over a pint.

## ⑫ Toner's★★
**139 Baggot Street Lower**
☎ 676 3090.

A marvellous, if slightly shabby pub with a worn bar, ageing wooden partitions, engraved mirrors, faded old advertisements and

countless little drawers dating from the time when it was a grocer's shop. It's the ideal place to come for an afternoon pint, where you can set the world to rights under the imperturbable eye of the barman. Yeats never set foot in a pub, apart from Toner's, where he would order a sherry.

## ⑬ Wellington Road★★

Of the many quiet streets in this smart district, this has the most rural air. Its rows of fine Georgian housess lined up behind green lawns, doors painted in different colours, and twin flights of steps evoke provincial calm rather than the busy feel of a capital city.

Shady pavements, English-style gardens filled with flowers, and a peaceful atmosphere sum up the old-fashioned charm of a district that's become one of the most expensive in Europe.

# Trendy Temple Bar district

Temple Bar, between the River Liffey and Dame Street, traditionally the banking street, was the port district in the 18th century. Ships docked at the quayside, and the Custom House was built here. Between the busy workshops and seedy hotels, the narrow cobbled streets were always thronged with people. After gradually falling into decay, the district has now been given a spectacular facelift. Music pubs, restaurants, street entertainers and discos make it the trendy place to be in Dublin after dark.

### ❶ Central Bank★

Dame Street.

Students of architecture, should visit this enormous cubic building, built in the 1970s. It's rather unattractive, but is interesting for its unusual construction. Built from the centre outwards, the floors were attached from the top downwards, beginning with the upper floors. The enormous cables are visible on the outside. The present building is actually a truncated version of the one originally envisaged.

### ❷ Foggy Dew★

1 Fownes St Upper
☎ 677 9328.

Behind a fine brick façade, this pub is full of nooks and crannies that give it a pleasant feel. You can order sandwiches from noon-6pm throughout the week (exc. Sun.), while listening to the sound of rock and pop or blues. On Sunday evenings there are concerts. The clientele is very varied.

### ❸ Sésí★

8 Crowe St (second-hand)
11 Fownes St Upper (designers)
☎ 677 4779.

Rummage around and you're sure to find what you're looking for among the jumble

### ❻ OLIVER ST JOHN GOGARTY★★★
**57 Fleet Street**
☎ **671 1822.**

The departure point of the Musical Pub Crawl, and one of the most popular pubs in the district, with its old-fashioned bar, tall barrels and live music daily. The best plan is to have bacon and cabbage or Irish stew for lunch here on Sunday between 12.30 and 2pm, during the traditional music concert. Guaranteed atmosphere for around IR£5/€6.

of second-hand clothes here, including traditional hand-knitted jumpers for IR£10/€13 and inexpensive outfits (from IR£25/€32) by young designers who are trying to make a name for themselves. The shop also has a range of natural incenses blended with essential oils to burn for every occasion, including an aphrodisiac.

### ❹ Hey! Doodle, Doodle★
**14 Crown Alley**
☎ **672 7382**
**Open Tue.,Thu.-Sat. 11am-6pm, Wed. 11am-9pm, Sun. 1-6pm (closed Mon.).**

Take a little time out being creative, or entertain the

children here with ceramics you decorate yourself. With a wide choice of designs starting from as little as IR£2/€2.50, you can afford to take some home as a souvenir of your visit. For the inclusive price of IR£5/€6, a piece is fired once you've finished decorating it, and sent on to you. The welcome is very friendly.

### ❺ The Auld Dubliner★★
**17 Anglesea Street**
☎ **677 0527.**

This is the place to come for an early-evening drink if you don't mind the crowds. It has a pleasant decor and you can have an inexpensive pub lunch here too.

Traditional music is played live from 9.30-11.30pm at the weekends (4-7pm weekdays), but you may find it rather touristy.

### ❼ The Temple Bar★★
**48 Temple Bar**
☎ **672 5286.**

One of the busiest pubs in the city, it's packed throughout the day with a motley crew typical of the city. Everyone

from *fashionistas* to old retainers, spill out on to the street on fine days and take over the pavement. The Temple Bar has the finest whiskey list you could wish for, with over 200 different varieties on sale. The pleasant little courtyard at the rear serves as a beer garden.

### **8 Original Print Gallery★**
4 Temple Bar
☎ 677 3657
**Open Tue.-Fri. 10.30am-5.30pm. Thu. 10.30am-8pm, Sat. 11am-5pm, Sun. 2-6pm.**

Here you'll find a wide choice of prints, drawings and paintings by contemporary Irish artists, from dark, abstract landscapes to more conventional pen-and-ink sketches. Prices start at IR£50/€63, and the shop can send your purchases home by post.

### **9 Irish Film Centre★★**
6 Eustace Street
☎ 679 5744
**Open every day 9am-11pm.**

Don't miss this place, even if you don't fancy seeing a film. There's an excellent cafeteria selling

delicious exotic dishes on the patio under the glass roof. The Dublin newspapers are available free here, use them to add the finishing touches to your plans for your stay. Gay publications are also on offer. If you're a keen film-fan, you can buy videos of all the most famous Irish films here, from *The Quiet Man* to *The Van* and *Waking Ned*.

### **10 Meeting House Square★**
Built on the former site of a Quaker meeting house, this little square behind the Film Centre is the venue for a local produce market every Saturday. From May to September a festival of free outdoor cultural events is held in the square, with performances of dance, theatre, opera and music and a 'Family Fun' programme of events on Sunday afternoons, with performers such as circus and mime acts. On Saturday evenings in summer, films are shown free on a giant screen above the Gallery of Photography (tickets allocated on a first come, first serve basis from the Temple Bar Information Centre).

### **11 Gallery of Photography★**
Meeting House Square
☎ 671 4654
**Open Tue.-Sat. 11am-6pm. Entry free.**

The ground floor has books, some of which are hard to find elsewhere, superb photos and original postcards and posters. The upper floors are devoted to exhibitions funded by the Arts Council. While international photographers are well represented, the emphasis is on high-quality contemporary Irish photography.

### ⑫ Design Yard★
**12 Essex Street East**
☎ **677 8453**
**Open Mon.-Sat. 10am-5.30pm, Tue. 11am-5.30pm.**

A centre of contemporary jewellery design, where an understated setting and cool music form the backdrop for a magnificent collection of jewellery made from gold, silver and semi-precious stones. Recycled materials, though less valuable, are also used to good effect.

### ⑬ National Photographic Archive★
**Meeting House Square**
☎ **603 0371**
**Open Mon.-Fri. 10am-5pm, Sat. 10am-2pm.**

Temporary exhibitions regularly mine the depths of the National Library, which stores over 300,000 drawings and photographs on every theme related to the history of the country. The archives can be accessed on microfilm by members of the public who wish to carry out research. For IR£5/€6.30 you can order a copy of any photo in the archive and

## ROCK TO THE RESCUE

The Temple Bar district almost disappeared in the 1980s. It became the insalubrious refuge of squatters and penniless artists, and was earmarked for demolition. However, the government intervened and came up with an ambitious renovation plan. This was backed by a number of artists, including U2, who bought the Clarence Hotel on Wellington Quay, and the fashionable club, now known as The Kitchen.

they will send it home to you by post.

### ⑭ The Porter House★★★
**16-18 Parliament St**
☎ **679 8847.**

A unique pub for the city, offering beer brewed on the premises. It's quite an achievement to be an independent brewer in

the home of the all-powerful Guinness brewery. Only the twelve home-brewed beers are served here, so there's no point in ordering a pint of the usual. If you're feeling adventurous, opt for tasters, so you can try them all, or just try Wrassler XXXX, which is every bit as good as Guinness.

### ⑮ Sunlight Chambers★
**Essex Quay.**

On the quayside, this façade stands out because of its neo-Romanesque windows and coloured high-relief friezes. The building dates from the early 20th century and was built by Lever Brothers, the manufacturers of Sunlight soap. The frieze tells the story of soap and its role in basic hygiene. In other words, it's a kind of educational comic strip.

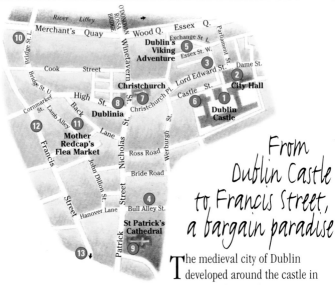

*From Dublin Castle to Francis Street, a bargain paradise*

The medieval city of Dublin developed around the castle in the direction of Christchurch. Further away, the Liberties district, was outside the city walls, and therefore not subject to its jurisdiction. Nowadays it's home to antique dealers, and at the weekend there's a small flea market. End a day of bargain-hunting by having a go at traditional dancing in one of Dublin's most authentic pubs.

### ❶ Dublin Castle★★
**Dame Street**
☎ 677 7129
**Mon.-Fri. 10am-5pm,
Sat.-Sun. 2-5pm.
Entry charge.**

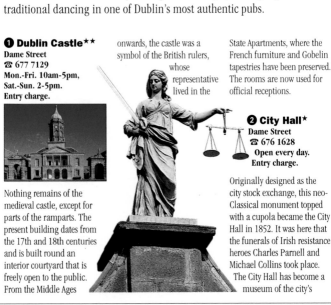

Nothing remains of the medieval castle, except for parts of the ramparts. The present building dates from the 17th and 18th centuries and is built round an interior courtyard that is freely open to the public. From the Middle Ages onwards, the castle was a symbol of the British rulers, whose representative lived in the State Apartments, where the French furniture and Gobelin tapestries have been preserved. The rooms are now used for official receptions.

### ❷ City Hall★
**Dame Street**
☎ 676 1628
**Open every day.
Entry charge.**

Originally designed as the city stock exchange, this neo-Classical monument topped with a cupola became the City Hall in 1852. It was here that the funerals of Irish resistance heroes Charles Parnell and Michael Collins took place. The City Hall has become a museum of the city's history and its people. The small café is run by the owners of the Queen of Tarts.

### ❸ Queen of Tarts★
**4 Cork Hill**
☎ 670 7499
**Open Mon.-Fri.
7.30am-6.30pm,
Sat. 9am-6pm,
Sun. 10am-6pm.**

An address for food lovers to remember, opposite the City Hall.

Sisters Regina and Yvonne are pastry cooks who collect delicious recipes. Their tarts and quiches, salads, cakes and muffins are irresistible. The Baileys cheesecake and apple and blackberry crumble are among the best on offer.

### ❹ Viking Splash★★
**Bull Alley Street (B3)**
☎ 855 2333
**16 Jun.-31 Aug.: every day
10am-5pm; Sep.-Oct.: Tue.-
Sun. 10am-5pm; Nov.: weekends only 10am-5pm (On
Sun. tours start 10.30am).**

A unique tour of Dublin by land and water in a WWII 'Army Duck'. Costumed and colourful guides trace Dublin's history from the first Viking settlement to the present day. The tour starts near St Patrick's Cathedral and ends in the Grand Canal Basin. Tour costs IR£10/€12.70 per adult.

### ❺ Dublin's Viking Adventure★
**Essex Street West**
☎ 679 6040
**Tue.-Sat. 10am-4.30pm, Sun
11am-4.30pm
Entry charge.**

You can discover the original Dublin founded by the

### THE VIKING PERIOD

Arriving in Ireland in the late 8th century, the Vikings are often credited with the founding of Dublin. They imposed their rule on the incumbent Celts, and embarked on raids throughout the island by making their way up the rivers. They gradually mingled with the local population and were finally integrated. A vast necropolis has been found in the Kilmainham district. The remains of the Viking settlement in Dublin were buried during the construction of the Civic Office, between the quays and Christchurch.

Vikings on board a longship. A reconstructed village complete with figures in period dress takes you back in time 1,000 years, with authentic sounds and smells to add to the realism of the scenes. It's a chance to find out about Viking customs, crafts and trade, and their conversion to Christianity.

### ❻ Whichcraft★★
**3 Castlegate**
☎ 670 9371
**Open Mon.-Sat. 9am-6pm,
Sun. 10am-6pm.**

Possibly one of the finest Irish craft shops in the city. The selection gives pride of place

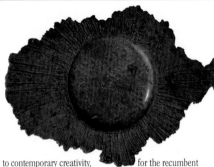

to contemporary creativity, freely inspired by Celtic tradition, with marvellous jewellery by Moritz Schurman and Vincent Meehan, elm dishes by David Comerford, and drawings by Gail Kelly. A second shop has recently opened in Cowes Lane.

### **7** Christchurch Cathedral★
**Christchurch Place**
**Open every day 10am-5pm.**
**Entry charge (free with the Dublinia tour).**

This Anglican church replaced the medieval one that disappeared long ago. The present building, dating from the 19th century, is a rather cumbersome mixture of neo-Gothic and neo-Romanesque styles. The crypt has remained intact since 1172. In the nave, look out

for the recumbent figure of Strongbow, a Norman who conquered the city in the 12th century.

### **8** Dublinia★
**Winetavern Street**
**☎ 679 4611**
**Open Apr.-Sep.: every day 10am-5pm; Oct.-Mar., Mon.-Sat. 11am-4pm, Sun. 10am-4.30pm.**
**Entry charge.**

An interactive trip through medieval Dublin by means of

wax models, reconstructions and everyday objects discovered in local digs. A tour of Christchurch is included in the entrance fee.

### **9** St Patrick's Cathedral★
**Patrick Street**
**☎ 475 4817**
**Open Mon.-Fri. 9am-6pm, Sat. 9am-5 pm, Sun. 10am-3pm (exc. during service 11am-12.45pm).**
**Entry charge.**

Visible from a distance with its tall steeple, St Patrick's is the

second medieval cathedral in the city and the most impressive. Legend has it that the patron saint of the country baptised the faithful here, on the very spot where he himself was converted, but the cathedral is now Anglican. Its most famous dean was Jonathan Swift, the author of *Gulliver's Travels*. The door of the south transept has a strange hole in it, so that two lords who didn't trust each other could shake hands and be reconciled without any risk.

### ⑩ The Brazen Head★★
**20 Bridge Street Lower
(Bus 21, 21A)
☎ 677 9549.**

There was already a coaching inn in this location in the 12th century, set back from the street. With its low beams, and worn bar and floors, today's pub oozes character. Irish nationalists, such as Parnell, O'Connell and Grattan, were all frequent customers. Although it's a tourist favourite, it's still a good place to come for pub food (served noon-10pm) such as Dublin coddle, or to listen to music in the evening.

soup at Mother Redcap's Tavern just next door, where there's live music every Sunday lunchtime.

### ⑪ Mother Redcap's Flea Market★★
**Back Lane
Open Fri.-Sun. 10am-5.30pm.**

A small flea market with all kinds of stallholders. There's plenty that's of little interest, and the jumble is indescribable, but you may just turn up an unusual souvenir for a reasonable price. In any case, it's all very good-humoured. After the bargaining, you can quench your thirst or enjoy a bowl of

### ⑫ Francis Street★
This long street is of little interest apart from its many antique shops. They aren't much to look at from the outside, but the items on offer inside are often fine quality and expensive. You may find just what you're looking for, but beware, many of the pieces are not genuinely Irish, but imported from England or from continental Europe. If you come away empty-handed you can console yourself with a snack

in the Gallic Kitchen (closed Sun.) at no. 49, which sells the most wonderful quiches and tarts, as well as delicious bread.

### ⑬ The Liberties★
To the east of St Patrick's Cathedral is a lively working-class district, with inexpensive shops, small markets and unpretentious pubs where local men meet regularly to talk. For bazaars and bargains of every kind, push on to The Coombe and Meath Street, before rejoining the north end of Thomas Street, where you'll find the College of Art and Design.

---

**A WORKING-CLASS DISTRICT**

Under English rule, Catholics were forbidden to come inside the city walls. They lived in misery, crowded together in tiny houses. The poverty of the urban architecture of the Liberties district is clear evidence of this difficult past. The present-day inhabitants, many of whom often work in the nearby breweries, still cling to their old traditions, representing the city as it was before the economic boom.

# Towards Phoenix Park, green and picturesque

The west of the city centre is traditionally a working area, with a large number of markets, distilleries and breweries. Beyond it, the vast green enclave of Phoenix Park, one of the biggest parks in the world, is the pride of Dubliners.

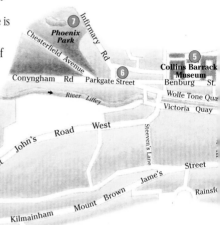

### ❶ Whiskey Corner★★
**The Old Jameson Distillery
Bow Street (buses 68, 69
and 79 from Aston Quay)
☎ 807 2355
Open every day 9.30am-6pm
Entry charge.**

The history of whiskey and a tour of the old distilleries, complete with synthesized smells, followed by a tasting of the different brands. The tour is interesting and there's also a shop where you can buy rare bottles and alcoholic souvenirs.

### ❷ Ceol★★★
**Smithfield Village
☎ 817 3820
Open Mon.-Sat. 10am-
5.30pm, Sun. 11am-5.30pm
Entry charge.**

This well-thought-out temple to traditional music is equipped with interactive terminals that seek to explain the island's musical history. There are hundreds of tunes to listen to, a fascinating film to see, and a good selection of CDs to buy. Allow at least an hour and a half here.

### ❹ Cobblestone★★
**77 King Street North
☎ 872 1799.**

This charming, if slightly dingy, pub has a village feel

that is typical of the district. A meeting place of horse traders and other locals, its impromptu musicians, lively

debates and endless pints of beer mean that it has plenty of atmosphere.

### ❺ Collins Barracks Museum★★
**Benburg Street
(bus 90 from Aston Quay or
172 from Kildare Street)
☎ 677 7444
Open Tue.-Sat. 10am-5pm,
Sun. 2-5pm
Entry free.**

Housed in an impressive barracks building dating from 1706, this annexe of the National Museum is devoted to popular art and traditions. Furniture, tools and everyday

objects recount the social history of the island. The top floor houses a display of 250 years of Irish jewellery and fashion, including an amusing perfume bottle with a periscope to help the owner look out for potential suitors. Cooke's Café offers delicious snacks in the courtyard.

### ❻ Ryan's ★★
**28 Parkgate Street**
☎ 677 6097.

With its fine Victorian panelling and stained-glass windows, this is one of Dublin's most photographed pubs. If you like your privacy, choose one of the snugs, small private compartments with a lockable door. Even better, they say that the barman

here pulls a perfect pint. The atmosphere is warm and inviting, particularly at the weekend. Food is served on the first floor.

### ❼ Phoenix Park ★
**Buses 25, 26, 66, 67 and 51.**

The green grassland and ancient trees of the biggest urban park in Europe (double the size of New York's Central Park) stretch to the west of the city. A zoo, the oldest cricket club in the country, polo pitches and the residence of the President of the Irish Republic are all to be found here.

### ❽ Kilmainham Gaol ★★
**Inchicore Road
(buses 51B, 78A and 79 from Aston Quay)
☎ 453 5984
Open Apr.-Sep., every day 9.30am-5pm, Oct.-Mar., Mon.-Fri. 9.30am-4pm, Sun. 10am-4.45pm.
Entry charge.**

Fans of Irish history will be fascinated by the tour of this prison, which closed in 1924. After a presentation of the nationalist movement and its heroes, you visit the two floors of cells, some of which were occupied by the great rebel leaders, and later by members of the IRA. The last of these prisoners was Eamon De Valera, the first Irish President.

### ❸ Smithfield Market ★★★
**First Sun. of the month.**

This colourful horse market is the last to be held right in the heart of a European capital. It's frequented by dodgy horse traders and kids who ride their horses bareback in the streets of the poorer suburbs. You'll find the atmosphere is quite unique, mainly because of the colourful characters that you come across.

### ❾ Guinness Storehouse ★
**St Jame's Gate
(buses 51B and 78A from Aston Quay and 123 from Cerys in O'Connell Street)
☎ 408 4800
Open every day 9.30am-5pm.
Entry charge.**

Above all a homage to the commercial side of the famous brewery, the tour explains the history of marketing the brand. The entrance fee is a bit expensive, even though you do get a pint of Guinness served at the bar.

# Rooms and restaurants
## Practicalities

## HOTELS

There are three levels of accommodation in Dublin, 1-4 star hotels, 1-4 star guesthouses (generally private houses that have been converted to receive guests and are midway between hotels and B&Bs), and bed and breakfasts, which some believe are the best way to see the Irish way of life. The centre of Dublin is small, and it tends to contain only the most luxurious hotels. Most of the guesthouses and B&Bs with character are a little way from the centre, but even the most distant are never more that 25 minutes walk from the centre and are close to a bus service. You'll find the least expensive accommodation north of O'Connell Street and in Drumcondra, towards the airport. The most pleasant district is south of St Stephen's Green and in the Ballsbridge area, where the guesthouses are elegant but more expensive. Remember that the best districts for nightlife are also the noisiest. The greatest attention is usually paid to decor and comfort in guesthouses and hotels, and hairdryers, kettles, and tea and coffee are provided. The most common decorative styles found in the hotels are English, Georgian or cottage-style. Breakfast, which is generally included in the price of the room, is a substantial meal, usually consisting of cereals, fruit juice, egg, bacon and sausages, tea or coffee, toast and preserves.

## PRICES

Inflation is a serious problem in Ireland, and prices have rocketed, especially in the capital. They vary little between summer and winter, but become almost prohibitive on St Patrick's Day and during the weekends of the rugby, hurling and football finals. The prices shown in brochures are generally per person, and include breakfast. However, those given here are for a double room with breakfast. A large number of hotels have special weekend offers that often include two nights and dinner. Expect to pay in the region of IR£200/€250 for a double room. You'll pay IR£120-150/€152-190 for a good hotel with character. To find this category of room for under IR£100/€127, you'll need to stay in the Merrion Square or Ballsbridge district in the south of the city. The least expensive accommodation north of the city centre costs in the region of IR£40-50/€51-63 staying in a B&B or guesthouse.

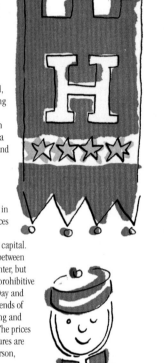

## RESERVATIONS

Dublin has relatively few rooms on offer to visitors. Whatever the time of year, don't try to come without booking in advance. Over Christmas and New Year, which are important family

and religious events in Ireland, many places of interest, as well as guesthouses and B&Bs, are closed. If you prefer, the tourist information office will take care of your reservations, and can be contacted by phone (☎ 00 353 1 605 7700) or via the Internet (www.visitdublin.com). Remember to state whether you want a double or twin beds. You'll always be asked to confirm by letter or fax and to send a deposit or credit card number.

## RESTAURANTS

Dublin has recently embraced international and exotic cuisine. And a good thing, too, since Irish cooking, apart from stews and simple fish dishes, tends to be fairly monotonous. The bill in the new restaurants can be quite hard to swallow, so take advantage of the sizeable breakfasts offered in the hotels and B&Bs, then have a hearty pub lunch. You'll be served pub food or a carvery lunch, including traditional dishes, such as bacon with cabbage, beef or lamb stew, a variety of roast meats, and so on. The pub is also the best place to meet people, since Dubliners rarely have lunch in a restaurant, as they tend to have their main meal in the evening. When it comes to dinner, try to stick to Irish time and eat early, between 6 and 7.30pm. Most restaurants have an 'early bird' menu that's cheap and filling. After that, you mainly order à la carte. Wine is pricey, and draught beer isn't served in restaurants because they haven't got the same licences as pubs.

### PRICES

You can get a very hearty pub meal at lunchtime for IR£6/€7.50. A pint of Guinness will cost you around IR£2.50/€3. In the evening, an 'early bird' set meal costs in the region of IR£12/€15 for three courses. An à la carte meal will cost IR£5-8/€6.50-10 for the starter, over IR£10/€12.50 for the main course, and IR£3-5/€4-6.50 for the dessert. It will say on the bill whether service is included or not. If it isn't, add 10% to the total. And never leave less than 50p/€0.65.

# HOTELS

## North of O'Connell Street

### Harvey's

**11 Gardiner Street Upper**
☎ 874 8384
**ᴳ** 874 5510
**Bus 41 (direct from airport)**
IR£50-80/€63-102.

A pleasant Georgian-style guest-house, with 16 rooms and the elegant decor of a family house. You'll feel at home as soon as you step inside. The bathrooms have bath-tubs, and the welcome is warm and enthusiastic. An excellent place to stay, only five minutes' walk from O'Connell Street. The hotel has a no-smoking policy.

### Carmel House

**16 Gardiner Street Upper**
☎ 874 1639
**ᴳ** 878 6903
**Bus 41 (direct from airport)**
IR£56-60/€71-76.

A charming, welcoming hostess and clean, comfortable rooms are the trump cards of this well-kept guesthouse with a traditional, slightly anonymous decor. The nine rooms offer very good value for money close to the city centre.

### Maple Hotel

**75 Gardiner Street Lower**
☎ 874 0225
**ᴳ** 874 5239
**Bus 41 (direct from airport)**
IR£60-70/€76-90.

A small hotel that's simple and comfortable close to the centre for a reasonable price. The ten rooms are all well equipped, with a hairdryer, TV and kettle for making tea. The decor is rather ordinary but tasteful.

### Lyndon House

**26 Gardiner Place**
☎ 878 6950
**ᴳ** 878 7420
**Bus 41 (direct from airport)**
IR£60-70/€76-90.

One of the fine Georgian houses in the district, well restored and turned into a nine-room family-run guesthouse. Bright colours add a cheerful note to the decor of each of the rooms. A thoroughly hospitable welcome less than five minutes on foot from O'Connell Street. Quiet and convenient.

## Drumcondra Road

**Buses 3, 11, 13A, 16, 16A, 33 and 41. Fare to city centre 85p/€1.08.**

### Tinode House

**170 Drumcondra Road Upper**
☎ 837 2277
**ᴳ** 837 4477
www.homepage.eircom.net/~tinodehouse
IR£55/€70.

A great B&B in a Victorian-style brick house that is covered in flowers in the spring. Overlooking the garden is a pretty veranda with comfortable sofas that invite you for a rest. The four pleasant rooms are tastefully decorated. Maureen and P.J. Dunne pay great attention to the service and go to great lengths to give you tips and suggestions to make your stay all the more memorable. One of the best hotels in the city at the price.

### Baldara

**126 Drumcondra Road Upper**
Iᴳ 836 8668
IR£50/€63.

A very pleasant B&B run by a delightful lady in one of the Victorian houses in the avenue. The six simple, well-equipped rooms are light and cheerful. Excellent value for money.

### Clareen House

**128 Drumcondra Road Upper**
☎ 837 1503
IR£55/€70.

This house, with its small English-style front garden, has four spotless and very comfortable rooms. A simple, restful setting and pleasant hosts make this high-class B&B a great place to stay.

## Along the Liffey

### Clarence

**6-8 Wellington Quay**
☎ 670 9000
**ᴳ** 670 7800
IR£210-475/€267-603 (plus breakfast IR£15/€19.

Taken over by the legendary rock group U2, and decorated in a contemporary style using marble, wood and leather, this 49-room hotel is one of the most luxurious places in Dublin. The rooms are furnished in light oak and leather, with sumptuous duvets covered in white linen. First-rate comfort and service, and a club (The Kitchen) and bar (The Octagon) that couldn't be smarter or trendier, plus a

famous Tea Room restaurant and an address on the edge of Temple Bar. Perfect for those who like to be seen in the right places.

## Morrison

**Ormond Quay**
☎ 887 2400
☎ 878 3185
www.morrisonhotel.ie
IR£250-450/€317-570

This fine, ultra-modern hotel with 95 rooms owes its decor to the Irish designer John Rocha, who came up with a restful mixture of Zen style and primitive art using luxurious materials. The rooms have high-tech facilities, light duvets and elegant bedlinen, from fine linen sheets to soft velvet bedspreads. The lounge overlooks the Liffey, with comfortable leather armchairs, and is a pleasant place to linger after shopping. The hotel is located just opposite Temple Bar, on the other side of Ha'penny Bridge.

## Isaac's

**Store Street**
☎ 855 0067
☎ 836 5390
IR£90-110/€114-140.

Behind Custom House, five minutes' walk from O'Connell Bridge, this former warehouse has been refurbished to become one of the most original hotels in the capital. With a flower-filled patio, cast-iron garden furniture, dining room with an amazing vault painted with foliage, and 58 very pleasant modern rooms, it offers some of the best value for money in the city.

## The Townhouse

**47-48 Gardiner Street Lower**
☎ 878 8808
☎ 878 8787
IR£50-80/€63-102.

A stone's throw from the main bus station, this elegant Georgian guesthouse is very competitively priced for the city centre. It's an excellent place to stay, with a turquoise floor and walls, and brightly-coloured posters in the welcoming lobby and elegant rooms that are either sober and very 'designer' or old-fashioned and cosy. The service is impeccable and in low season there are sometimes offers of a third night free; check when you book.

## Abbey Hostel

**52 Abbey Street Middle**
☎ 872 8188
☎ 872 8585
IR£90-120/€114-152.

Half-way between O'Connell Street and Temple Bar, this small hotel with 21 well-equipped rooms has a classic English decor, consisting of dark panelling and striped or tartan curtains. The bar is warm and convivial, with soft lighting and wood panelling.

## Harding

**Fishamble Street**
☎ 679 6500
☎ 679 6504
IR£64-69/€81-88.

A slightly impersonal modern hotel with 53 light, brightly-decorated rooms offering every comfort. Overlooking Christchurch, it's close to the centre, but away from the hustle and bustle making it a convenient place to stay. Breakfast isn't included in the price, which is, nevertheless, very competitive (full Irish breakfast IR£5.95/€7.50, continental IR£3.95/€5.00.

## Earl of Kildare

**Kildare Street**
☎ 679 4388
🅕 679 4914
**IR£50-70/€63-90.**

A super hotel with loads of character right next door to Trinity College. The bar is really lovely and is entirely covered in portraits of Irish politicians. It's very popular with MPs on weekdays, when they're sitting in the nearby Parliament. The practical, traditional rooms have all mod cons, including a TV, hairdryer and kettle. It's a quiet, unpretentious place, and you can eat very well in the bar.

## St Stephen's Green and Merrion Square

### The Merrion

**Merrion Street Upper**
☎ 603 0600
🅕 603 0700
**www.merrionhotel.com**
**IR£240-800/€305-1,016.**

Unquestionably the smartest and most luxurious hotel in the capital, the Merrion combines old Georgian Dublin charm and elegance with the most modern facilities and an incomparable air of quiet luxury. The birthplace of the Duke of Wellington, it boasts lounge after lounge filled with the best private Irish collection of paintings as well as crystal chandeliers, fireplaces and moulded ceilings, an 18th century-style garden, a Louis XIV dining room and a vaulted stone wine cellar. It also has one of the best restaurants in the country, and several bars, as well as an indoor swimming pool and a fitness centre.

## Browne's Townhouse

**22 St Stephen's Green**
☎ 638 3939
🅕 638 3900
**www.brownesdublin.com**
**IR£155-175/€197-222.**

This guesthouse, opposite St Stephen's Green, has 12 rooms each more cosy than the last, decorated in a 19th-century English manor-house style, with rich, wine-coloured hangings, mahogany furniture and chandeliers. A peaceful, elegant enclave in the heart of the city, where the welcome and service guarantee a perfect stay. Some of the rooms have four-poster beds, and you can also ask for a suite, although it will cost more.

## N° 31

**31 Leeson Close**
☎ 676 5011
🅕 676 2929
**www.number31.ie**
**IR£110-180/€140-229.**

One of the city's best places to stay, just three minutes' walk south of St Stephen's Green, discreetly hidden behind a large gate. The combination of fine Georgian residence and courtyard, with an annexe with light, contemporary architecture, adds up to an unusually charming hotel. With French period furniture, silky fabrics in sherbet colours, and carpets in rich shades, it's quite irresistible.

## Merrion Square Manor

**31 Merrion Square**
☎ 662 8551
🅕 662 8556
**IR£100-110/€127-140.**

A splendid residence decorated in period style in the heart of the Georgian city. Old furniture, crystal chandeliers and heavy hangings re-create the elegant atmosphere of 18th-century

Dublin. Brocades, plain velvet and floral prints alternate to good effect. Each of the 22 rooms is decorated in a different colour, and has a charm of its own. Just opposite Merrion Square and its large park, with Grafton Street only five minutes' walk away.

### Baggot Court

**92 Baggot Street Lower**
☎ 661 2819
✆ 661 0253
**IR£100-110/€127-140.**

This very quiet house, with double-glazing on the street side and a sober, restful decor, is close to the centre in the Georgian district. The rooms have all mod cons, and the most expensive also have a kitchenette. Five minutes from St Stephen's Green.

### Ballsbridge

**Buses 5, 6, 7, 8 and 45**

### Butler's House

**44 Lansdowne Road**
☎ 667 40 22
✆ 667 3960
**IR£150/€190.**

Behind its discreet façade, this small luxury guesthouse has 19 very elegant rooms. A great deal of care has been taken over the Victorian decor, comfort and service. The lounge is especially appealing. With its deep sofas, vast book-covered coffee table and generous floral displays, it's a combination of luxury and elegance. Look out for their special weekend offers, which include free tickets for the theatre.

### Lansdowne Manor

**46-48 Lansdowne Road**
☎ 668 8848
✆ 668 8873
**www.lansdownemanor.ie**
**DART station Lansdowne Road**
**IR£100/€127.**

This elegant guesthouse consisting of two Victorian manor houses side by side has 23 rooms furnished in the purest late19th-century British style, with floral hangings, wing chairs and mahogany furniture. The vast lounge and some of the rooms have bow windows. The guesthouse is situated in the embassy district in the south of the city, 25 minutes' walk from the centre.

### Raglan Lodge

**10 Raglan Road**
☎ 660 6697
✆ 660 6781
**IR£80-110/€102-140.**

This large family house, built in 1860 on a fine, tree-lined avenue combines the imposing facade, dark wood and cosy atmosphere of the Victorian era. Each of the eight elegant rooms has its own particular charm, with high ceilings and large windows. One of the best places to stay, where visitors are received in style. Fifteen minutes' walk from Grafton Street.

### Glenveagh House

**31 Northumberland Road**
☎ 668 4612
✆ 668 4559
**Buses 6, 7, 7A, 8 and 45**
**IR£80-90/€102-114.**

A large, classically elegant family house on a shady avenue 15 minutes' walk from the centre. With its pastel colours and dark wood, it's very British in style . The rooms at the back of the house are the nicest.

### Lansdowne Villa

**10 Lansdowne Terrace**
**Shelbourne Road**
☎ 668 8905
✆ 668 5302
**Buses 6 and 7 or DART Lansdowne Road**
**IR£65/€83.**

This simple little house tucked away behind well-trimmed hedges is a rare B&B in an expensive district. It's very well kept, with seven enormous, light rooms and all mod cons at unbeatable prices. The rates go up when the rugby and football finals are being played in the nearby stadium.

# RESTAURANTS

## Around O'Connell Street

### Chapter One

**18-19 Parnell Square**
**☎ 873 2266**
**Open Tue.-Sat. 12.30-2.30pm, 6-10.30pm, closed Sat. lunch., Sun. and Mon.**

Subtle, elegant cuisine served in a pretty basement dining room with stone walls, sizeable pictures and deep sofas where you can sip an aperitif before your meal. Once you've taken in the pleasant decor, sit back and enjoy lightly-cooked Mediterranean vegetables, delicious grilled fish, fresh cod braised with vegetables or scallops roasted with bacon. Expect to pay around IR£18/€23 at lunchtime and IR£38/€48 in the evening, unless you eat the excellent pre-theatre set meal for IR£20/€25 before 7pm.

### 101 Talbot

**101 Talbot Street**
**☎ 874 5011**
**Open Tue.-Sat. 5-11pm, Fri. noon-11pm.**

This first-floor restaurant is attractively decorated with large, colourful paintings, and is one of the nicest in Dublin, offering a pleasantly relaxed atmosphere, young, enthusiastic service and well-cooked international cuisine. You could try the fillet of salmon grilled in a herb crust, barbecued tuna or a tasty filo parcel stuffed with goat's cheese, brocoli, leeks and peppers. The main courses cost around IR£10-13/€13-17. Draught Guinness is on offer here.

## Along the Liffey

### Caviston Seafood Bar

**Epicurian Food Hall, Liffey Street**
**☎ 878 2289**
**Open Mon.-Sat. noon-5.30pm.**

An original way to eat seafood, sitting at the bar, close to the stalls of this pleasant food arcade. Caviston's also has a restaurant at the side, which offers a few simple, delicious dishes. It's the ideal place to lunch on grilled prawns in spicy sauce, smoked salmon with dried tomatoes and feta, or freshly-caught crab with mayonnaise. Many of the dishes are under IR£7/€9.

### Arnotts Studio Bar

**Abbey St Middle/Henry St (several entrances) (C2)**
**☎ 805 0400**
**Open Mon.-Sat. 9am-5.30pm, Thu. 9am-9pm, Sun. noon-6pm.**

Located on the second floor mezzanine, this airy coffee shop is lit by the store's giant glass cupola. You can watch the shoppers come and go on several floor levels around you. Light continental cuisine for breakfast and lunch. Expect to pay IR£1.50-3.25/€1.90-4.13 for breakfast and IR£3.50-5.50/€4.45-7 for lunch. Try the smoked salmon pannini with Cashel Blue cheese (£5.50/€7).

## Trinity College

### Beshoff

**14 Westmoreland Street**
**☎ 677 8026**
**Open Mon.-Sat. 10am-11pm, Sun. noon-11pm.**

This old-fashioned fish and chip shop is a Dublin institution. It's a hundred years old, and still has its original black and gold shop front, high ceilings and black marble table tops. You can eat here for less than IR£5/€6, choosing from a wide variety of fish, as well as the inevitable sausages, burgers and chicken.

### Nude

**21 Suffolk Street**
**☎ 677 4804**
**Open every day 8am-10pm.**

A healthy, eco-friendly fast-food

restaurant serving dishes to take away or eat at long communal tables surrounded by benches. Help yourself to salads, low-fat, organic desserts and delicious fresh fruit and vegetable juice from the buffet before going to the counter to order home-made soups served with fresh bread or wraps, hot or cold pancakes, rolled and stuffed with exotic spicy mixtures. A filling snack costs around IR£5/€6.

### Grafton Street

## Stag's Head
**Dame Court**
**☎ 679 3701.**

Many Dubliners agree that this is the best pub to have lunch. It's certainly a great place to try bacon and cabbage or a generous helping of traditional meat and two veg. Look out for the mosaic of a stag's head, the emblem of the house, on the ground in front of the entrance. The same motif appears on the engraved mirrors and stained-glass windows of the long room inside. The varied, colourful clientele only adds to the charm of the place.

## QV2
**14-15 St Andrew Street**
**☎ 677 3363**
**Open Mon.-Wed. 6-11pm, Thu.-Sat. noon-3pm, 6pm-midnight.**

High-quality and traditional cuisine in a peaceful setting, with plenty of space between the tables. For lunch, you could try Eoin's fish pie (fish and prawns with a crispy topping) or corned beef with a leek and spinach crumble. In the evening, the choice might include Lamb Daniel Patrick or Barbary duck. Early-bird rates apply from 6-7.30pm. Otherwise, expect to pay IR£8-10/€10-12.70 at lunchtime and IR£12-16/€15-20 in the evening.

## Fresh
**Powerscourt Townhouse Centre, top floor (C3)**
**☎ 671 9669**
**Open Mon.-Sat. 10.30am-5pm.**

This cheerful self-service vegetarian restaurant offers hot dishes, salads, gourmet sand-wiches, juices, smoothies and lassis. It's worth noting that they also cater for a range of special diets: some of the cakes and confectionery, for example, are yeast, gluten or sugar-free. The Lebanese courgette and chickpea filo pie, and the leek, onion and blue cheese tart are well recommended. Sandwiches start at IR£2.50/€3.20, hot dishes cost IR£6.10/€7.75 (including two side salads).

## Mao
**2-3 Chatham Row**
**☎ 670 4899**
**Open Mon.-Fri. noon-10.45pm, Sat.-Sun. noon-10.30pm.**

This Chinese restaurant, where you can order with your eyes shut and be sure of eating something delicious, already has a good reputation. The flavours of the produce are respected, and the food is cooked to perfection. It's frequented by a young clientele throughout the day – be prepared to queue occasionally in the evening and at lunchtime. For lunch, make do with a starter, such as the copious chicken lemongrass salad, and dessert (all for under IR£8/€10). In the evening, try the more elaborate dishes, such as Malaysian chicken or crispy duck (Peking duck and Chinese noodles), for IR£8-10/€10-12.70.

## Cooke's Café
**14 William Street South**
☎ 679 0536.

A trendy restaurant where you may bump into passing celebrities. The ground floor is informal and fashionable, and people eat here to see and be seen. Mediterranean salads are served with tasty home-made bread, and there are also seafood dishes, including mussels. For dessert, the hot pear and raspberry tart is a treat. On the first floor, the Rhino Room, with its pseudo-Gothic decor,

serves equally accomplished Mediterranean-style cuisine, but it's available only for private hire. Expect to pay IR£18-25/€23-32 for lunch and over IR£25/€32 for dinner.

### Temple Bar

## Irish Film Centre
**6 Eustace Street**
☎ 679 5744.
**Open Mon.-Sat. 9.30am-11.30pm, Sun. 9.30am-11pm.**

Midway between a pub and a restaurant, this is a favourite, with its glass-roofed patio and bistrot tables. Cheap, appetising dishes include well-seasoned warm chicken, stuffed peppers and hearty *stoemp,* a mixture of potatoes, sausages and bacon for cold days. All the dishes cost under IR£7/€9, and there's also Guinness on draught.

## Eamon Doran's
**3A Crown Alley**
☎ 679 9773.

This convivial restaurant, housed on the first floor of a former warehouse, has a few rustic tables and a very long bar. The good plain home cooking may be uninventive, but it's served in generous portions, with folk and blues music in the background. The early-bird set meal at under IR£10/€13 is very good value. Otherwise the dishes cost around IR£7-8/€9-10.

## Bad Ass Café
**Crown Alley**
☎ 671 2596
**Open every day 11.30am-midnight.**

A great place for students, those on a budget and families, in the heart of Temple Bar. The food mainly consists of pizzas, salads and pasta, with lunchtime specials at affordable prices (IR£4.95/€6.25, 11.30am-4.30pm) and all kinds of theme specials, from Mexican to Italian to Cowboy. Sinéad O'Connor worked here as a waitress before she

became rich and famous. You'll always find lots of artists and musicians here, soaking up the atmosphere.

### Dublin Castle Francis Street

## Yamamori
**71-72 South Great Georges Street**
☎ 475 5001
**Open Mon.-Wed. 12.30-11pm, Thu.-Sat. 11am-12.30pm.**

This large, uncluttered Japanese restaurant, with its modern decor and very good music, is increasingly fashionable with young Dubliners. It offers meals at a wide range of prices, including Chinese noodles in all kinds of sauces, and chicken, seaweed and vegetables of every kind, as well as more elaborate sushi. Expect to pay IR£7-12/€9-15.

## Leo Burdock's
**2 Werburgh Street**
☎ 454 0306
**Open every day noon-midnight.**

This cult restaurant serves some of the best fish and chips in the city. The long queue that stretches along the pavement even when it's raining is proof enough. It offers a number of different kinds of fish, all served with chips, which can be cooked crispy on request. You can eat them, like everyone

else, in the cathedral garden opposite. Under IR£4.50/€5.70 for large cod and chips.

## The Gallic Kitchen

**49 Francis Street**
☎ 454 4912
**Open Mon.-Sat. 9am-5pm.**

A delicatessen, bakery and small café rolled into one, The Gallic Kitchen is well known to gourmets, who buy their delicious bread here. You can also try fresh vegetable or cheese quiches, salads and very rich chocolate cakes at the counter along the wall. If you didn't find anything you liked in the local antique shops, you could always take home some of the home-made chutneys, sauces, jellies and jams on sale here.

### Georgian districts

## Restaurant Patrick Guilbaud

**21 Merrion Street Upper**
☎ 676 4192
**Open Tue.-Sat. 12.30-2pm, 7.30-10.15pm.**

Patrick Guilbaud, considered to be the best chef in Dublin, runs this restaurant, located on the ground floor of the smart Merrion hotel. The dining room is particularly elegant, decorated with fine paintings by the Pont-Aven school. The French cuisine is faultless, even if some customers and critics say it lacks charisma. The foie gras, lobster and local lamb won't disappoint, but the bill will be well in excess of IR£70/€90 for dinner and IR£22/€28 for lunch.

## L'Écrivain

**109a Baggot Street Lower**
☎ 661 1919
**Open Mon.-Sat. 12.30-2pm, 7-11pm, closed Sat. lunchtime and Sun.**

One of the most refined restaurants in the capital, L'Écrivain affects a smart French style that's much in favour in Dublin. The decor naturally has a literary theme, with a statue of Brendan Behan and portraits of famous Irish writers. The restaurant serves balanced cooking that makes good use of seasonal produce from the market. Lamb, fish, game and original desserts are served with great professionalism. Try the baked rock oysters, York cabbage and crusty cured bacon. Early-bird IR£17.50/€22, lunch IR£17-20/€22-25, dinner IR£35/€44 table d'hôte.

## Pier 32

**23 Pembroke Street Upper**
☎ 676 1494
**Open every day 12.30-2.30pm, 6.30-11pm.**

A former cellar with stone walls decorated as a seascape, with fishing nets, lobster baskets and lifebuoys. A guitarist and soft lighting create a cosy atmosphere. The authentic cuisine is directly inspired by classic Irish country dishes that exploit fresh produce to advantage. The seafood and lamb are particularly well prepared. Depending on the amount you order, expect to pay IR£12-20/€15-25.

## Ely

**22 Ely Place**
☎ 676 8986
**Open Mon.-Sat. noon-midnight.**

A delightful wine bar that also serves meals throughout the day, from snacks and traditional dishes at lunchtime to more refined cuisine in the evening. Only organic produce is used, and the wine list has over 80 different bottles listed (some of

which can be ordered by the glass). For a change from formal meals, try the duck salad with cashew nuts, followed by a selection of Irish cheeses. In the daytime, ask for one of the small tables on the mezzanine in front of the window. The dishes vary in price from IR£5/€6 to IR£13/€17. A glass of wine costs IR£3.60-16/€4.50-20.

# Shopping Practicalities

The shops in Dublin are concentrated in fairly small areas, making it easier to plan a shopping trip. With a large number of cafés and pubs scattered across the city centre, you shouldn't have far to look for a break and some refreshment either.

## WHAT TO BUY IN DUBLIN

The items most frequently bought by visitors to the Irish capital are traditional knitwear and crystal.

The keynote of Irish style is understatement. As far as clothes are concerned, you can safely fill your suitcases

Book lovers are bound to find what they're looking for in the big, well-stocked bookshops of the capital, and given the city's literary background, you're sure to be inspired to catch up on your reading.

These timeless classics are high-quality articles which, though relatively expensive, never go out of fashion and give years of use. In recent years, designers such as John Rocha, Paul Costelloe and Louise Kennedy have given traditional Irish knitwear and tweed clothing an exciting contemporary treatment, whilst some of these designers have also turned their hand to creating new lines in elegant crystal glassware.

with Aran sweaters, tweed jackets, scarves, wraps and linen garments.

When it comes to interior decoration, linen tablecloths and napkins are a safe bet, as are the wool or mohair throws. If you're looking for up-to-the-minute fashion, Irish designers will not disappoint. They are available in stores listed throughout the following pages.

Lovers of traditional music can take the opportunity to buy CDs that simply can't be found elsewhere.

Last but not least, food lovers should make a beeline for the sauces and condiments, toffees, chocolates, teas, coffees, whiskey-flavoured marmalades and biscuits. Spirits are very heavily taxed but many visitors still choose to take home an authentic bottle of Irish whiskey.

# WHERE TO SHOP

Although it's Ireland's capital, Dublin is more like a country town in size and has few shopping areas. Generally speaking, the department stores and inexpensive shops are found on the north bank of the Liffey. The smart shops tend to be concentrated to the south of the river. The department stores – Clery's on O'Connell Street, and Arnott's, Debenham's, Marks & Spencer and Dunnes Stores on Henry Street – offer a very wide choice of goods (fashion, interior decoration, accessories and so on) at reasonable prices.

Henry Street is where you'll also find trendy Irish shops, such as Sacha and A-Wear, as well as the high-street regulars such as Next and Oasis and the very cheap shops favoured by teenagers. Earl Street North is the home of the bargain stores. The best high-quality craft shops are next to Trinity College in Nassau Street. The smartest fashion shops are in Grafton Street and neighbouring streets, especially the Powerscourt Townhouse Centre. On the corner of St Stephen's Green, the shopping centre of the same name also houses a multitude of shops.

# SHOP OPENING TIMES

The shops are open Monday to Saturday from 9am-5.30 or 6pm. Thursday is late closing day, when the shops shut at 7.30 or 8pm. Shops usually stay open at lunchtime. If you want to shop on Sunday, go to Grafton Street, where most of the small shops are open from 11am or noon until 5.30 or 6pm. All shops close on Easter Day, 25 and 26 December and St Patrick's Day. Most stay open on other public holidays.

# METHODS OF PAYMENT

All the shops take credit cards, most commonly Visa and Mastercard. American Express isn't so widely accepted. Some of the shops use manual machines to swipe your credit card, so make sure that no extra sheets have been placed under the slip to duplicate your card number. The amount is then written in by hand, so check it's correct before signing, and make sure you keep your copy. Some tourist shops take traveller's cheques but the exchange rates aren't very good. Change them at the bank and then pay cash.

# DUTY-FREE PURCHASES

Travellers from countries outside the EC can claim back the VAT (17·36%) on goods they buy. State that you want a tax refund when making a purchase and produce your passport. The shopkeeper will then fill in a form specifying the type of article and its price, which the purchaser must present to customs on leaving Ireland. The duly stamped document should then be sent back to the shopkeeper, who will refund the VAT.

## FINDING YOUR WAY

After the address of each entry in the Shopping and Nightlife sections, a grid reference is given in brackets which refers to the map of Dublin on pages 82-83.

# SENDING GOODS HOME

The best tourist shops are happy to send goods by post or courier, as appropriate. Fragile objects can be expensive to insure, so ask for details before going ahead with your purchase.

# CUSTOMS

Since Ireland is part of the EC, you no longer have to declare your purchases if you live in a member state. For further information see p. 7.

## FINDING A BARGAIN

Don't try to haggle in Dublin; it just isn't done, except when something is faulty. If you're hoping to find a bargain, come during the sale season, in January or July, when big reductions (up to 60% off) can be had in most of the shops. In-between times, especially in May, you can also take advantage of the mid-season sales. The discounts may be smaller, but there are still plenty of bargains to be had.

# WOMEN'S FASHION

When it comes to fashion, Dublin is a place of paradox. The great classics, such as oilskin jackets, tweeds and knitwear – the basics in every wardrobe – sit side by side today with creations by young Irish designers who aim to give tradition an imaginative twist.

### The Design Centre
**Powerscourt Townhouse Centre, 2nd floor (C3)**
**Open Mon.-Sat. 10am-6pm,**
**Thu. 10am-8pm,**
**Sun. noon-6pm.**

This is the ideal place to discover Irish designers. There are beautiful, elegantly simple clothes in linen, wool and silk (nothing under IR£100/€127), knitted outfits with pure lines and in soft colours (around IR£200/€250), and smart, fluid dresses for the tall and slender (up to IR£600/€760). The knitwear by Lainey Keogh and the collection by Lyn Mar are quite irresistible.

### Platform & Eile
**50 William Street South (C3)**
**☎ 667 7380**
**Open Mon.-Sat. 9.30am-6pm, Thu. 9.30am-8pm.**

An arched laneway shop that's ultra-smart and trendy, with tables covered in beautiful accessories adjacent to the clothes rails. Take a look at the knitwear by the Irish designer Deirdre Fitzgerald and funky Irish designer Talula de la Lune. There's also a wide choice of clothes by the Irish designers Jacob Tutu, Elva Robins and Tim Ryan knitwear. Despite the wide range of prices, you should expect to pay IR£100/€127 for a dress.

### Costume
**10-11 Castle Market (C3)**
**☎ 679 4188**
**Open Mon.-Sat. 10am-6pm, Thu. 10am-7pm.**

A mecca for fashion victims, this shop naturally sells the Costume brand designed and made in Dublin, as well as clothes by

## LINEN SECRETS

Irish linen is a classic fabric. To whiten yellowed linen, use peroxide rather than bleach. Dry it in the sun to make it even whiter. Never wring wet linen, and iron it while it's still damp – more effective than steam. If you haven't time to do the ironing when the linen is damp, wrap it in plastic and leave it in the refrigerator. (for no longer than 24 hours). Only iron dark colours on the back, and don't put the clothes away in piles that are too tightly packed, as linen easily becomes mildewy.

Spanish designer Custo (colourful little tops), Italian designer Luciana Zuffi, English designer Joelynian, and Irish designer Leigh Tucker. Prices in the range of IR£50-350/€63-445).

### Kilkenny Centre

5-6 Nassau Street (C2-C3)
☎ 677 7066
Open Mon.-Sat. 9am-6pm,
Thu. 9am-8pm,
Sun. 11am-6pm.

Among the more traditional items, keep an eye out for creations by the younger generation of Irish designers. One of the best is Louise Kennedy, who combines perfect cut, natural fabrics (linen, silk and wool) and simple lines (over IR£150/€190). You'll also love the designs by Aideen Bodkin, and clever, stylish knitwear and bags by Orla Kiely. Also look out for Kilkenny's stylish own label. There's also a menswear department.

### Vivien Walsh

24 Stephen Street (C3-B3)
☎ 475 5031
Open Mon.-Sat. 10am-6pm
(Thu. until 7pm).

You'll find exquisite fashion and accessories here, as well as Vivien Walsh's own internationally acclaimed jewellery – pretty pieces in antiqued metals and Swarovski crystals (IR£25-£250/€32-317). The shop specializes in small unusual designer collections – little stretch muslin tops (from IR£100/€127), shoes by Gianni Barbato (from IR£140/€178) and Jamin Peuch beaded and embellished bags (from IR£175/€222), as well as very individual scarves.

### Gibson Price

17 Suffolk Street (C2)
☎ 677 7436
Open Mon.-Sat. 9.30am-6pm, Thu. 9.30am-8pm.

In this shop you'll find smart casual wear for women of all ages, characterized by superb cut and fabrics such as fine wool, tweed and cashmere, as well as linens and cottons in summer. Labels include Sand and Wellington. Look out for stylish wrap-over tops (IR£70/€90) and dressy white trousers (IR£110/€140).

### Debenhams

Jervis Shopping Centre
Jervis Street (B2)
☎ 878 1222
Open Mon.-Fri. 9am-6pm,
Thu. 9am-9pm, Sat. 9am-6.30pm, Sun. noon-6pm.

Like its English counterpart, this department store offers a wide choice of clothes at all prices, but the Dublin branch does have a few surprises in store. Creations by the Irish designers John Rocha and Louise Kennedy are particularly well represented. Don't miss the accessory department, where you're sure to fall for a bag by Lulu Guinness or a fabulous hat by Philip Treacy.

## Air Wave

36 Grafton Street (C3)
☎ 679 8374
Open Mon.-Tue. 9.30am-
6pm, Thu. 9.30am-8pm,
Sun. 2-6pm.

A shop for men and women,
selling clothes by many of latest
designers. For women, there's
Marina Avraam and her gypsy and
hippie-inspired clothes, Resource,
August Silk and In Wear. The
stock changes frequently, and
everything is bang up to date.
Prices start at IR£50/€63.

## Avoca

11-13 Suffolk Street (C2)
☎ 677 4215
Open Mon.-Sat. 10am-6pm;
Thu. 10am-8pm.

The eclectic mini department
flagship store of Avoca
Handweavers stocks desirable
items from Ireland and all around
the world. The Avoca Collection
includes traditional elegance with
suits and coats in wool and linen
mixes woven at the Avoca Mill,
which is the oldest working mill
in Ireland, dating from 1723.
Hope + Thimble, their younger
line, has a romantic individual
look with embellished individual
pieces. You'll find signature vests
(IR£39/€50), double faced
linen jackets, dainty wraparound
cardies and a variety of skirts
and beautiful coloured lace
aprons for going out.

## Brown Thomas

92 Grafton Street (C3)
☎ 605 6666
Open Mon., Tue. 10am-
6.30pm, Wed., Fri.,
Sat. 10am-
7pm, Thu.
10am-8pm,
Sun. noon-
6pm.

Brown Thomas is Dublin's most
upmarket department store, with
the best of Irish and international
design on offer. Here you'll find
Lainey Keogh, Paul Costelloe,
Louise Kennedy, Quin & Donnelly
side by side with Prada, Dries van
Noten, Marnie, Max Mara, Joseph
and other stars of the design
constellation. Terrific shoes, bags
and scarves – and a wonderful
cosmetic hall.

## Blue Eriu

7 William Street South (C3)
☎ 672 5776
Open Mon.-Sat. 10am-6pm,
(Thu. until 8pm),
Sun. 2-6pm.
Salon: Mon.-Fri. 9.30am-
8pm, Sat. 9.30am-6pm,
Sun. 2-6pm.

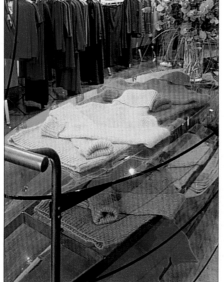

International beauty with a Celtic flavour, inspirational cosmetics and luxurious treatments. This very trendy beauty retreat also has a treatment room in the Clarence Hotel. Facials by Eve Lom and Dr Haushka with products from Chantecaille, Nars, Shu Uemura, Sundari and Kiehls. Scents by Aqua di Parma. Book well in advance for treatments. Expensive but worth it.

### Louise Kennedy

**56 Merrion Square (D3)**
**☎ 662 0056**
**louisekennedy@eircom.net**
**Open Mon.-Fri. 9am-6pm,**
**Sat. 9.30am-6pm.**

Louise Kennedy is regularly hailed as one of Ireland's leading designers, with a devoted clientele which includes former president of Ireland, Mary Robinson and Cherie Blair, wife of the British prime minister. Her distinctive,

well cut clothes are made in soft tweeds, cashmere and angora wools. Look for short fitted tweed jackets (from IR£350/€445), beaded evening dresses (from IR£500/€635), large cashmere shawls (from IR£300/€380), and sparkly corsages (from IR£35/€44), as well as a great range of coats and separates. You'll also find bags by Lulu Guinness and Osprey, and hats by Philip Treacy. In the giftware department look for her airy crystal glasses and pale blue or chocolate brown candles (from IR£12/€15).

### Rococco

**1 Westbury Mall (C3)**
**☎ 670 4007**
**Open Mon.-Sat. 10am-6pm, Thu. until 8pm.**

Rococco stocks small quantities of unusual labels, with an emphasis on pretty, whimsical clothes. The pieces work together both for day and evening with layering, embroidered detail and natural fabrics. Look out for Irish jewellery by Catriona Hayes for her label Mes Rêves, and the delicate work of Elva Robins.

### Susan Hunter

**13 Westbury Mall (C3)**
**☎ 679 1271**
**email: suhu@indigo.ie**
**Open Mon.-Sat.**
**10am-6pm.**

A fabulous little lingerie shop bedecked in jewel-coloured silks and beloved of rock stars and the visiting glitterati. They stock all the big names such as La Perla, Aubade, Lejaby and Hanro,

## CLOTHES AND SHOE SIZES

Sizes for clothes and shoes in Dublin are the same as in the UK. If you require any further help you'll find a handy conversion table on page 126.

but look out for the Irish range, Rapture – pure silk gowns, pyjamas, nightdresses and camisoles (from IR£65/€83) in ivory, pale pink or red.

## A Wear

**26 Grafton Street (C3)**
**47 Henry Street (C2)**
**☎ 671 7200**
**Open Mon.-Sat.**
**9.30am-6pm, Thu.**
**9.30am-8.30pm,**
**Sun. noon-6pm.**

A Wear is a label much loved by the young, for its prices, its range of matching accessories, and its knack of always coming up with tomorrow's fashions. Its designs allow youngsters to follow the dictates of fashion without breaking the bank, with lots of colourful little dresses (from IR£22/€28) and three-quarter sleeve shirts. The shop also sells an exclusive, affordable line by the well-known Irish designers Quin & Donnelly, including linen suits and smart separates (from IR£60/€76). Keep an eye out for the in-house label 'A-Design'.

## Dunnes

**St Stephen's Green Shopping**
**Centre (C3)**
**☎ 478 0188**
**(Branches also in Grafton**
**Street and Henry Street)**
**Open Mon.-Sat. 8.30am-7pm**
**(Thu. until 9pm), Sun.**
**noon-6pm.**

Dunnes is the Irish equivalent of Marks & Spencer. A great value chain store whose own label, St Bernard, covers everything from the hottest fashion trends to more conservative clothing. With an excellent range of linen dresses, duster coats and pastel trousers for spring and summer and real value in winter woollens. Great underwear, children's, men's and home-ware lines, too.

## FIRST AID FOR MATTED PULLOVERS

If you find your favourite pullover's become matted after it's been washed a little too vigorously, there's no need to panic. Soak it in water for two days, then wash by hand with soap flakes. After rinsing carefully, leave to soak for the rest of the day in a solution of tartric acid (8 spoonfuls to 2 litres/3¹/₂ pts of water). Rinse carefully and dry flat.

### Thomas Patrick

**77 Grafton Street (C3)**
**☎ 6713866**
**Open Mon.-Sat. 9.30am-6pm, Thu. 9.30am-8pm.**

For stylish, classic footwear in a variety of fine leathers, this shop is a must. You'll find a strong Italian influence with brands such as Magli and di Sandro, but the overall effect is of contemporary elegance in both the formal and more casual ranges. There's also an equally well-stocked men's department.

### Pia Bang

**46 Grafton Street (C3)**
**☎ 671 5065**
**Open Mon.-Sat. 10am-6pm, Thu. 10am-8pm, Sun. 2pm-6pm.**

With a sharp, sculpted image, this long-established shop updates its stock every few weeks. Excellent for different styles of trousers (from £90/€114), little wrap-around blouses (from £85/€108), silk dresses and linen suits (from £360/€457). There's a shoe department on the mezzanine, with dainty shoes from £60-£250/€76-317, as well as a good selection of evening wear and accessories (from £250/€317).

### Buffalo Boots

**16 Exchequer Street (C2)**
**☎ 671 2477**
**Open Mon.-Sat. 10am-6pm, Thu. 10am-8pm.**

You'll find the most amazing shoes here, including fluorescent sheepskin clogs, disco-style sequinned trainers (IR£100/€127), brightly-coloured trainers with platform soles

(IR£100/€127), and summer flip-flops (IR£20/€25). Obviously, the louder the better here. Some of the styles are hilarious – guaranteed to get you noticed.

## ACCESSORIES AND JEWELLERY

Whether it's a smart hat or a precious piece of contemporary jewellery, you'll find what you need in Dublin to add a touch of individuality to your outfits. Give a new twist to classic leather gloves by choosing them in orange or lime green. Choose diamonds in a modern setting of yellow and white gold or do the rounds of the second-hand shops to unearth an opulent 1930s necklace.

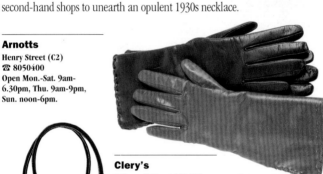

### Arnotts

**Henry Street (C2)**
☎ 8050400
**Open Mon.-Sat. 9am-6.30pm, Thu. 9am-9pm, Sun. noon-6pm.**

### Clery's

**O'Connell Street (C1-C2)**
☎ 878 6000
**Open Mon.-Wed. and Sat. 9am-6.30pm, Thu. 9am-9pm, Fri. 9am-8pm.**

Give a plain outfit a lift with a coordinating hat, scarf, gloves and even tights. You'll find a dazzling array of colours on the ground floor of Clery's department store. The gloves come in ultra-soft leather in acid colours, embossed velvet and Lycra (from IR£15/€20). There are tights and shoes to match (from IR£5/€6) just across the aisle.

Arnotts is Ireland's oldest and largest department store, with frontage on three of Dublin's busiest streets – Henry Street, Abbey Street and Liffey Street. With a huge selection of every imaginable kind of accessory for the fashion conscious, look for belts, hats, throws, bags etc. by Irish designers including John Rocha, Michael Mortell, Michel Ambers (you'll find the accessories displayed alongside the clothes). This is one of the best places to find that elusive piece which finishes an outfit.

### Rhinestones

**18 St Andrew Street (C2)**
☎ 679 0759
**Open Mon.-Sat. 9.30am-6pm, Thu. 9.30am-8pm, Sun. noon-5pm.**

This shop stocks lovely old costume jewellery, made mainly of silver and semi-precious stones. Elaborate, and even extravagant, compositions, of the type that were popular between the wars, and in the 1950s. The collections contain appealing. From the simplest of rings to the most imposing of necklaces, there's something to suit every purse.

### The Steensons
**16 Frederick Street South (C3)**
☎ 672 7007
**Open Mon.-Sat. 10am-5.30pm.**

Bill and Christina Steenson, originally from Northern Ireland, are among the most creative jewellers in the country. For the last twenty years or so, they've produced innovative contemporary designs based on

period pieces, and are tastefully presented (prices start at IR£50/€63).

### New Moon
**28 Drury Street (C2-C3)**
☎ 671 1154
**Open Mon.-Sat. 10am-6pm, Thu. 10am-8pm, Sun. noon-6pm.**

A shop selling costume jewellery and accessories in a wide variety of ethnic-inspired styles. The Celtic designs, based on interlacing knots and spirals, set with large chunks of amber and coloured stones, are particularly

age-old Celtic patterns. The result is starkly beautiful original jewellery in which yellow or white gold is combined with precious stones to produce bold and highly elegant compositions.

### Michael Perry
**Powerscourt Townhouse Centre (C3)**
☎ 677 6781
**Mon.-Sat. 10am-6pm, Thu. 10am-8pm.**

It's worth visiting this jeweller's just for the pleasure of seeing him at work behind his window. You'll see him handling precious metals with dexterity to make modern jewellery that's both

## WRAPPING IT UP

The scarf has always been a staple of a woman's wardrobe and, in recent years in Ireland, it has enjoyed a huge surge in creativity – particularly in worked and expensive fabrics. These new creations can be better described as throws or wraps, as the headscarf is no longer worn as a fashion statement. They are worn around the neck as a shawl, to decorate a jacket or to cover the shoulders in a gauzy film. Look out for Louise Kennedy's magnificent cashmere or silk wraps, Avoca's textured wool pleated scarves and Lorraine Bowen's collection in velvet or worked felted wool. Brown Thomas has a breathtaking selection arranged in colour gradations.

refined and elegant. He combines the different-coloured golds to manufacture simple, harmonious designs that contrast sharply with over-elaborate traditional jewellery. Fine chokers, pendants, earrings and rings are presented in a clean, contemporary idiom.

# MEN'S FASHION

Dublin's best buys for men are traditional clothes, such as tweed jackets, coats, shirts and pullovers. As the American influence becomes more and more marked, the city's shops also stock styles from the other side of the Atlantic, from East Coast preppie to denim-clad cowboy.

### Louis Copeland

**39-41 Capel Street (B2);
18-19 Wicklow Street;
30 Pembroke Street Lower
☎ 872 1600
Open Mon.-Sat. 9am-
5.30pm, Thu. 9am-8pm.**

Considered to be one of the best tailors in Europe, Louis Copeland makes suits to measure from IR£600/€760 according to the fabric.

For this, you'll get the ultimate in suits, and the tailor will keep your measurements on his books in order to serve you better in the future. In the area of ready-to-wear, he stocks a selection of brands, such as Valentino, Brioni, Canali and Ralph Lauren. For a local maker, plump for the Irish house Magee. Besides its famous tweeds, it offers a range of surprisingly elegant suits in fine wool (IR£449/€570) or linen for the summer. Alterations can be done in a trice.

### Thomas Pink

**29 Dawson Street (C3)
☎ 670 3720
Open Mon.-Sat. 9.30am-
6pm, Thu. 9.30am-8pm.**

It may come as a surprise, but the men behind Thomas Pink are actually Irish. The Mullen brothers set out in 1984 to conquer the English shirt market. At this well-known tailor's the walls are lined with shirts of every kind – striped, plain and checked, in traditional fabrics, such as Oxford cloth, poplin, twill and cambric (from IR£55/€70), all perfectly cut, down to the smallest detail. Accessories include elegant cufflinks, collar stiffeners and silk ties (from IR£39/€50). A room at the back of the shop is reserved for women's blouses (from IR£59/€75).

### Alias Tom

**Duke Lane (C3)
☎ 6715443
Open Mon.-Sat. 9.30am-
6pm, Thu. 8.30am-8pm.**

In this wonderful men's shop they boast that they can dress anybody from head to toe. You'll find the best international labels, from Prada sunglasses to Burberry luggage and the service is very attentive – staff, while not being intrusive, are ready to help customers put an entire look together. Suits from IR£175-1,500/ €222-1,905; shoes IR£69-330/ €88-420; ties from IR£30/€38.

## BT2

**28 Grafton Street (C3)**
☎ **605 6666**
**Open Mon.-Sat. 10am-6.30pm, Thu. 10am-8pm, Sun. noon-6pm.**

This annexe of the smart Brown Thomas department store is the haunt of young Dubliners on the lookout for trendy casual wear. Nothing too extravagant, just big international brands, at the same price as anywhere else, including

Polo Sport by Ralph Lauren, French Connection, Tommy Hilfiger, Calvin Klein, Armani, DKNY Jeans and Prada. Especially interesting during the sales period.

## Guinness Store

**34 Grafton Street (C3)**
☎ **670 8864**
**Open Mon.-Sat. 9am-6pm, Thu. 9am-8pm, Sun. noon-6pm.**

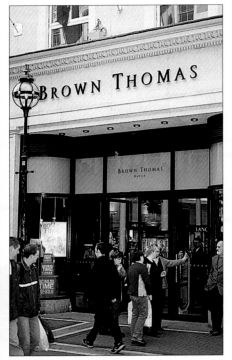

### CAP OR HAT?

A tweed cap or hat is the perfect souvenir to bring back from Ireland. But which? There are two schools of thought in the matter. The cap is virtually the national emblem, while a hat offers better protection from the rain. What's really important is the quality of the tweed, which must be tightly woven and crease-resistant, so you can stuff it in your pocket and then put it back on your head without looking like a tramp.

This shop pays homage to the famous Dublin stout, with embroidered polo shirts, T-shirts, caps and sweaters, as well as other memorabilia, such as ties sporting rows of pints. Prices start from IR£9/€11.

### Kevin & Howlin

**31 Nassau Street (C2-C3)**
☎ 677 0257
**Open Mon.-Sat. 9.30am-5.30pm.**

This family-run business is the home of the best-quality Donegal tweed, a place where you can dress from head to foot in the fabulous woollen fabric. The tweed comes in many different subtle patterns, colours and txtures, but the high quality and the hard-wearing and crease-resistant texture remain the same. Expect to pay around IR£65/€83 for a waistcoat, IR£215/€273 for a jacket, IR£285/€362 for an overcoat, and IR£25-35/€32-44 for a cap or hat. However, as they'll last a lifetime, it will be money well spent.

### Kennedy & McSharry

**39 Nassau Street (C2-C3)**
☎ 677 8770
**Open Mon.-Sat. 9am-5.30pm, Thu. 9am-8pm.**

A traditional shop, selling quality Irish and international menswear. Established in 1890, Kennedy & McSharry has a fine selection of hand-woven Donegal tweed jackets and warm Henry White overcoats and duffle coats, wool and cotton cable stitch sweaters

(IR£80/€102), soft Jonathan Richards scarves (IR£39.50/€50), and traditional caps and hats. It also has a selection of original, hand-painted ties by Véronique Didi, a Belgian living in Ireland, who uses Celtic themes as a source of inspiration and interprets them in a range of soft colours (IR£39.50/€50).

### Denim Bar

**10 Earl Street North (C1-C2)**
☎ 872 4377
**Open Mon.-Sat. 9am-6pm, Thu. 9am-8pm.**

A shop that sells nothing but jeans of every conceivable make and style— stonewashed, faded, classic, straight-legged, baggy or flared. The prices are more or less the same as anywhere else – IR£43/€55 for 501s, and IR£33/€42 for Wranglers. However, the choice is vast, and, with regular discounts and special offers, such as two for the price of one, there are definitely bargains to be had.

### Monaghans

**15-17 Grafton Arcade (C3)**
☎ 677 0823
**Open Mon.-Sat. 9am-6pm, Thu. 9am-7.30pm.**

Monaghans is situated in the Royal Hibernian Way Shopping Mall, in the arcade that runs between Dawson Street and Grafton Street. If you like soft, warm jumpers, you're sure to find something worth buying here. Don't expect anything too

### CLOTHES AND SHOE SIZES

Mens clothes and shoe sizes in Ireland are the same as in the UK. However, for those travellers unfamiliar with this system there are conversion charts on p. 126 for further information.

revolutionary, however; everything here is classic and timeless, including Pringle cashmere sweaters, Nautica jackets and Karl Lagerfeld jeans. The traditional Aran sweaters in pure cashmere are worth a special mention. Expect to pay in the region of IR£300/€380.

## Mister Gear

**14 Earl Street North (C1-C2)**
**☎ 874 2129**
**Open Mon.-Fri. 9.30am-6pm, Sat. 9am-6pm.**

An amazing shop straight out of Texas, with every possible accessory for the urban cowboy, from leather boots lacking only spurs to classic or brightly-coloured Stetsons, some decorated disco-style with sequins. If you see yourself as Davy Crockett, you'll find fringed waistcoats and jackets here (from IR£100/€127) and trousers to match, as well as T-shirts, embroidered shirts, lace ties, bandanas and scarves in garish, multi-coloured prints, and belt buckles in the form of Indian heads, eagles and lions (from IR£10/€12.50). Just perfect for all those line-dancing sessions.

## Kapp & Peterson

**117 Grafton Street (C3)**
**☎ 671 4652**
**Open Mon.-Sat. 9am-5.30pm.**

This smokers' shop sells pipes made by traditional methods, that require a very slow seasoning. Expect to pay a minimum of IR£20/€25 for a pipe, bearing in mind that the finest cost up to IR£200/€250. Non-smokers with a fondness for Swiss knives can see the whole range of accessories here.

## J. J. Fox Ltd

**119 Grafton Street (C3)**
**☎ 677 0533**
**Open Mon.-Fri. 8.30am-5.30pm, Sat. 9am-5.30pm.**

Specializing in cigars tobacco and pipes, this shop stocks a whole host of accessories of every kind for smokers and pipe lovers, and sells a variety of loose tobacco mixtures as well as a range of original silk ties and a selection of fine wines.

# CHILDREN'S CLOTHES AND TOYS

Although few Irish designers have developed a range of children's clothes, you'll find plenty to please the youngsters in Dublin. Go for the fun items that children love or reproductions of antique toys.

### Baby Bambino
**41 Clarendon Street (C3)**
☎ 671 1590
**Open Mon.-Sat. 10am-6pm,
Thu. 10am-7pm.**

Gorgeous array of designer children's wear, with everything to dress your child from birth to age 16 (girls), or age 12 (boys). All the top selling labels are here, including Charabia, Baby Dior, Gianfranco Ferre and Joseph. Don't miss the lovely knits from the latter (IR£50/€63 upwards). If you want to bring home a very special gift, look out for the simple and beautiful Irish christening robes in linen and organza by Glen Craft (IR£140-190/€178-240).

### Arnotts
**Henry Street**
☎ 805 0400
**Open Mon.-Sat. 9am-6.30pm, Thu. 9am-9pm, Sun. noon-6pm.**

This is a mecca for the fashion-conscious child. Virtually every leading label is here – Elle, Diesel, Lego, Tommy Hilfiger, DKNY, Timberland, Kookai, etc. Irish brands are well represented too, and you can also kit your baby, child or teenager out in everyday basics. The funky Impulse section will appeal to older teenagers.

### J. F. K. Sports
**3 Mary Street (B2)**
☎ 872 6215
**Open Mon.-Sat. 9.30am-5.30pm.**

Sporty parents and children alike will love this narrow shop. It isn't much to look at from the outside, but it hides an incredible variety of children's sports shoes. Even babies in their cradles can wear tiny Nikes, Reeboks, Filas and other famous streetwear names, while there are adorable black patent-leather trainers for little girls, and mini-sports shoes just like dad's for boys (from IR£20/€25).

## The Model Shop

**13 Capel Street (B1-B2)**
☎ 872 8134
**Open Mon.-Sat. 9.30am-5.30pm.**

If you like miniature cars, this is the place to come to find a miniature taxi or bus complete with advertisements of the kind found on the streets of London and Dublin during the 19th century. With all the fire engines, postal vans, delivery vans bearing Irish household names, cars of all makes and models, and motorbikes of every kind on offer, you'll be spoilt for choice. Older children will also find amazing collections of lead soldiers that are exact replicas of the regiments that made European history.

If your kids like collecting spin-offs from American films or television series, give them a treat by bringing them along to this shop, which sells the most amazing toys and gadgets. The PC Zone department will please fans of video games.

## The Dolls Store

**62 South Great Georges Street (B3)**
☎ 478 3403
**www.dollstore.ie**
**Open Mon.-Sat. 10am-5pm.**

Dolls and dolls' houses, those symbols of Victorian England, please little girls and collectors alike. This shop will take you back to your childhood, with a range of child-high dream

### Teddies galore

A shop for teddy lovers, with bears of all sizes and masses of clothes and accessories. From pocket-sized teddies to big softies to snuggle up to in the evening, customers are spoilt for choice at T. Bear & Co., on the ground floor of St Stephen's Green Shopping Centre (C3) (☎ 478 1139, open Mon., Wed. and Sat. 9am-6.30pm, Thu.-Fri. 9am-7pm, Sun. 2-6pm).

## Smyths Toys & PC Zone

**Jervis Street (B1-B2)**
☎ 878 2878
**Open Mon.-Sat. 9am-6pm, Thu. 9am-9pm, Sun. 12.30-6pm.**

houses to assemble yourself (IR£120-375/€152-476 according to model and size), a choice of furniture, wallpaper, and accessories to decorate them with, and dolls from a bygone age to inhabit them (IR£40-200/€50-250 for collector's items). If you're on a budget, it also offers a range of miniature teddy bears (from IR£5/€6) and the doll's hospital can repair your broken treasures.

# INTERIOR DECORATION

Dublin has some surprises in store for amateur interior decorators. Look for small specialist shops. The bigger, more expensive stores tend to be too traditional, or only sell imported articles rather than Irish products. Some department stores, on the other hand, have tasteful, inexpensive pieces, though they're often surrounded by tacky items.

### Foko
**66 South Great Georges Street (B3)**
☎ **475 5344**
**Open Mon.-Sat. 9.30am-6pm, Thu. 9.30am-8pm, Sun. 2-6pm.**

From kitchen and bathroom gadgets to contemporary furniture, Foko has everything you need to decorate your home in a young, relaxed style. If there isn't much room in your suitcase, look at the Beatles musical boxes, the matt silver Japanese mesh lanterns (IR£30/€38) or even a novelty bath kit (from IR£33/€42).

### Stock
**33-34 King Street South (C3)**
☎ **679 4316**
**Open Mon.-Sat. 9.30am-5.45pm.**

You'll see a few tempting items of furniture here, but Stock is mainly worth visiting for its utensils and kitchen objects. Gourmet cooks come here for

cake tins of every shape and size, including a very practical cylindrical bread tin for making round loaves (IR£6/€7.50), and handy utensils, such as vegetable graters and tools for piercing eggs without breaking them. Don't miss the range of strong wicker storage baskets either.

### The Drawing Room
**29 Westbury Mall (off map)**
☎ **677 2083**
**Open Mon.-Sat. 10am-6pm, Thu. 10am-7pm.**

Tasteful objects for fans of Georgian and Victorian decor – ornate mahogany frames, knick-knacks, embroidered cushions,

and lamp bases made from Chinese porcelain, in unusual shades such as soft yellow, or in wood, richly decorated with monochrome painting, elephants, cats or floral motifs. Expect to pay at least IR£100/€127 for a lamp.

### Knobs and Knockers
**19 Nassau Street (C2-C3)**
☎ **6710288**
**Email: info@knobsandknockers.ie**

This architectural ironmongery store has everything you could possibly want in door furniture, from letter plates (IR£15-115/

€19-146) to Georgian style knockers (£12-150/€15-190). The Irish Claddagh knocker, based on the symbolic

'friendship, loyalty and love' Claddagh ring, is a big seller (from £20/€25). They also stock an eclectic range of nautical giftware, from model boats to porthole mirrors (£20-£600/€25-760).

## Capsule

**26 Westbury Mall (off map)**
**☎ 672 5379**
**Open Mon.-Sat. 10am-6pm,**
**Thu. 10am-7pm.**

An interesting selection of beautiful objects that are all very modern but have no real practical use when it comes to decorating your home, including pebble candleholders, graceful glass

bud vases, pretty frames, electronic gadgets, and quite a collection of amusing mini-clocks in all different shapes and styles. Gifts at all prices.

## Empires

**14 Westbury Mall (off map)**
**☎ 679 2197**
**Open Mon.-Sat. 10am-6pm,**
**Thu. 10am-7pm.**

A small shop specializing in oriental carpets, with over 1,000 examples in stock. The carpets, which come from Turkey, Iran and Afghanistan, are priced from IR£100-1,500/€127-1,900 each, according to size and design.

### A QUESTION OF STYLE

Interior decoration is a hobby that is becoming popular world-wide. Four broad trends of interior style can be seen in Dublin's shops. The Georgian style, with its Classical rigour and strict, austere lines, blends well with the city's architecture and involves conservative, heavy hangings and lots of plain fabrics and stripes. The Victorian style combines mahogany and elaborate floral patterns, lace and flounces, ornaments and elaborate lamps. The more rural cottage style repeats the flowers, but with a preference for chintz over brocade and antique pine to dark, polished woods. Lastly, contemporary furniture, inspired by the designs of Terence Conran and John Rocha, uses pale woods such as beech and light oak contrasted with satin-finish metal and pure lines.

The tightly-woven kilims are really lovely, with a fine palette of muted shades and complicated patterns.

### Candleberry

**Westbury Mall (C3)**
☎ 671 8441
**Open Mon.-Sat. 10am-6pm, Thu. 10am-7pm.**

If you love romantic evenings dining by candlelight, or are simply stuck for an unusual or original gift to take home, there's a veritable cornucopia of candles in this pleasant shop. They come in all shapes, sizes and perfumes – with vanilla the top seller. Candleberry also sells a range of candle accessories – candelabras, candlesticks and candle holders –

in a variety of styles from traditional to contemporary. The beautiful packaging and wrapping service make this the ideal gift stop.

### The Ha'penny Bridge Galleries

**15 Bachelor's Walk (C2)**
☎ 872 3950
**Open Mon.-Sat. 10am-5.30pm.**

This antique dealer on the banks of the Liffey, has a definite leaning towards bric-à-brac, though he sometimes has a few fine pieces in stock depending on local sales and deliveries. It's worth keeping an eye out for fine antique desks, Victorian console tables, side tables, old advertisements and china.

### Giles Norman Photography Gallery

**Powerscourt Townhouse Centre (C3)**
☎ 677 3455
**Open Mon.-Sat. 10am-6pm, Thu. 10am-8pm, Sun. noon-6pm.**

This young photographer from Kinsale, on the south coast of Ireland, has made a name for himself with black-and-white landscapes that perfectly capture the island's melancholic charm. The catalogue alone is worth keeping (IR£18/€23), and all the photos can be sent unframed to your home address (from IR£20/€25 to IR£70/€90). He has some effective night-time shots of Dublin pub fronts.

Dunnes Stores is the Irish version of Marks & Spencer, selling good-quality bed linen, curtains, cushions and wooden accessories, including picture frames, at competitive prices. The crockery, which is either brightly coloured or discreetly simple, is also worth a look There's something to suit all tastes at very modest prices.

## S. F. Cody's Emporium at Arnotts

**12 Henry Street (C2)**
☎ **872 1111**
**Open Mon.-Sat. 9am-6.30pm, Tue. 9.30am-6.30pm, Thu. 9am-9pm, Sun. noon-6pm.**

In the basement of Arnotts department store, an entire section devoted to designer objects and the American way of life, based on rough-hewn wood, natural fabrics and china. Between the interior decor and cookery books, which are full of great ideas, and the items for the home (photo holders, knick-knacks, and bath salts and soaps with evocative names), it's hard to know what not to buy.

## Dunnes Stores

**Henry Street (C2)**
☎ **671 4629**
**Open Mon.-Sat. 9am-6pm, Thu. 9am-9pm.**

## Murphy, Sheehy & Co

**14 Castle Market (C3)**
☎ **677 0316**
**Open Mon.-Fri. 10am-5.30pm, Sat. 10am-5pm.**

A marvellous jumble of rolls of material of every kind, including woollen, linen and cotton furnishing fabrics, both rustic and elegant. Try the Foxford tweeds (Donegal, IR£10/€12.70 yd) or wool and mohair mixtures (IR£8/€10 yd) to make unusual throws for your sofas, or curtains to keep out the draughts. The 36in wide tweed is really good value at only IR£4.50/€5.70 per yard and the heavy linens (IR£8-15/€10-19 yd in extra wide widths) and damasks can be made into long-lasting tablecloths, and will only improve their appearance with age. Among the table linen, the napkins (IR£3/€3.80 each) and linen-cotton mixture tea towels (IR£2/€2.50) are a bargain.

## TRADITIONAL CRAFTS

There are many shops in Dublin specializing in knitwear, tweed and crystal, the work of Irish craftsmen and women. Be on your guard, however. The worst is often sold alongside the best, and the quality varies enormously. There are undoubtedly bargains to be had, but the genuine article, although expensive, is made to last a lifetime.

and christening robes. Ladies' fine wool capes start from IR£190/€240. You can also find tablecloths and napkins in 100% Northern Irish linen here, as well as the Irish version of Dresden-style china figurines, including a delicate collection in shades of blue.

### Kilkenny Centre
**5-6 Nassau Street (C2-C3)**
☎ 677 7066
**Open Mon.-Sat. 9am-6pm, Thu. 9am-8pm, Sun. 11am-6pm.**

### Blarney Woollen Mills
**21-23 Nassau Street (C2-C3)**
☎ 671 0068
**www.blarney.ie**
**Open Mon.-Sat. 9am-6pm, Thu. 9am-8pm, Sun. 11am-6pm.**

The Dublin outlet of the famous County Cork spinning mills offers some of the best choice of traditional shopping to be found, with pullovers, jackets and hats, as well as pretty Irish lace, a speciality of the west coast town of Kenmare (doilies and box covers from IR£4/€5), children's clothes

Dublin's most prestigious traditional shop sells an incredible range of timeless products (including hand-made Aran sweaters from IR£90/€114), with a touch of creativity added by young designers. Knitwear is given a fresh slant in cotton (from IR£40/€50), linen and silk, and the tweeds have a couture air about them. On the home front, fine china has been dropped in favour of rustic pottery, such as the country-motif earthenware by Nicholas Mosse. Celtic spiral motifs adorn the blue and yellow pots of the Brandon Pottery, with mugs from IR£5/€6.

### Kevin & Howlin
**31 Nassau Street (C2-C3)**
☎ 677 0257
**Open Mon.-Sat. 9.30am-5.30pm.**

Unquestionably the best place in Dublin to buy men's jackets (IR£215/€273), women's jackets (IR£195/€247) and Donegal tweed waistcoats. You can be sure of the cut and

the quality, and can choose from herringbone, mottled tweed, and small hound's-tooth checks in blended shades produced by natural dyes. You can buy hand-woven matching tweed by the metre (IR£19.50/€24.50 per metre in a 75cm width), to make a skirt, for example. Caps and hats are available in the same fabrics.

## The House of Ireland

37-8 Nassau Street (C2-C3)
☎ 671 1111
www.houseofireland.com
Open Mon.-Sat. 9am-6.30pm, Thu. 9am-8pm, Sun. 10.30am-5.30pm.

Aran sweaters for men, made by hand with the name of the knitter on a label (round neck IR£90/€114), or machine-made, in a soft mixture of alpaca and wool (IR£60/€76). Hand-made children's knitwear starts at IR£35/€44, and Donegal caps cost IR£21/€26. Besides these basics, there's a good selection of crafts and luxury goods, such as china and crystal.

## Dublin Woollen Mills

41 Ormond Quay Lower (B2-C2)
☎ 677 5014
www.woollenmills.com
Open Mon.-Sat. 9.30am-6pm.

This shop has been run by the same family for four generations, and tradition takes pride of place. The goods on offer — Aran sweaters, scarves, tweed hats, skirts and jackets — couldn't be more classic. The wide range of materials include cashmere,

## HAND OR MACHINE?

When buying tweed or knitted garments, always read the label carefully, and don't be led astray by the word 'hand', which means different things in different contexts. With knitwear, you need to distinguish between 'hand-knitted', which means made by a knitter using knitting needles, and 'hand-loomed', which means made by someone manually operating a knitting machine. Apart from the labelling, there's a difference in the appearance, too. Hand-knitted garments are thick, and often quite stiff and when they are held them up to the light, thet appear very dense. Machine-made garments are more loosely knitted, more supple, and allow more light through. Hand-knits are more expensive, but warmer and never lose their shape. With tweed, 'hand-woven' refers to traditional weaving on a hand loom. The fabric comes in narrow widths, and is stiff and very tightly woven, which is a sure sign of quality.

cotton, linen and lambswool. Pure wool plaids by John Harly are good value, with prices starting at IR£22.50/€28.50 for small sizes.

## Clery's

O'Connell Street (C1-C2)
☎ 878 6000
Open Mon.-Wed. and Sat. 9am-6.30pm, Thu. 9am-9pm, Fri. 9am-8pm.

with crystal from Waterford and Tipperary. Check out designer Paul Costelloe's new range of plain ceramics for Wedgwood (from IR£40/€51 for a jug, bowls fromIR£15/€19). Two talented Irish designers have recently created new lines for the traditional factories. John Rocha, for Waterford, has come up with minimalist forms inspired by the curves of the landscape (*Incline Geo* vase IR£110/€140, dish IR£100/€127). For Tipperary, Louise Kennedy favours spirals

The department in the basement offers a wide range of traditional Irish products, from the most tacky souvenirs to fine, elegant crystal. Wool plaids by John Hanly come in subtle shades of grey, beige, sky blue and pale yellow (IR£35/€44 for the medium size), while Foxford plaids are available in fluffy beige and navy mohair (IR£45/€70). You'll find scarves made of pure wool or wool and cashmere blends from IR£10/€13, and novelty ties for those who like Celtic motifs or Guinness.

## Brown Thomas

**88-95 Grafton Street (C3)**
**☎ 605 6666**
**Open Mon.-Sat. 9am-6pm, Thu. 9am-8pm, Sun. noon-6pm.**

The tableware department at this Dublin institution is well stocked

In this shop you'll find a range of ultra-conservative but high-quality traditional clothes, knitwear in a good choice of patterns and tweed jackets and capes of every colour. Prices are similar to those in the other shops.

## The Donegal Shop

**St Stephen's Green Shopping Centre (C3)**
**☎ 475 4621**
**Open Mon., Wed. and Sat. 9am-6pm, Thu.-Fri. 9am-8pm, Sun. noon-6pm.**

that reflect the light (IR£29/€37 for a glass).

## Triona Design

**Powerscourt Townhouse Centre (C3)**
**☎ 670 5989**
**www.trionadesign.com or www.eiremall.com**
**Open Mon.-Sat. 10am-6pm, Thu. 10am-8pm, Sun. noon-6pm.**

This is one of the best places in the city to buy machine-made Aran sweaters that keep their shape well

(from IR£30/€38). The prices are the same for hand-knits as you'll find elsewhere. Tweed jackets made from hand-woven Magee tweed from Donegal start at around IR£150/€190 and the inventive knitted hats created by a young designer on sale here are both warm and elegant (prices from IR£20/€25).

### Inish
**11 Lord Edward Street (C2)**
☎ 679 0665
**Open every day 10am-6pm.**

A privately-owned boutique selling lots of pretty items, including inexpensive Celtic jewellery in various styles (brass brooches for around IR£10/€13, sweaters from IR£29.50-90/€37.50-114). In the basement, you'll find original cashmere and linen hand-made scarves IR£15-50/€19-63) that you won't find elsewhere.

### The Crafts Centre of Ireland
**St Stephen's Green Shopping Centre, top floor (C3)**
☎ 465 4526
**Open Mon.-Sat. 10am-6pm, closed for lunch 2-3pm**

This store has a wide selection from leading Irish craft workers, in such different materials as glass, ceramics and textiles. While the traditional classics are represented, the emphasis is on top contemporary design – Jerpoint Glass, Dublin Ironcraft, Michael Kennedy ceramics, Valerie McCrudy scarves, etc. Check out the Celtic wall hangings.

## MUSIC AND BOOKS

How could you visit Dublin without bringing back a book or some music, the two great passions of the Irish, whatever their social background? Whether you want to tackle Joyce or discover contemporary writers, or buy the latest Chieftains CD or a Celtic harp, allow some time to explore the city's record shops and bookstores.

### The Celtic Note
**14-15 Nassau Street (C2-C3)**
☎ 670 4158
**Open Mon.-Sat. 9am-6.30pm, Sun. 9.30am-5.30pm.**

A great shop for music lovers, who can listen to CDs here before buying them, which is unfortunately rare in Dublin. The wide choice of sounds on offer extends beyond the purest forms of traditional music to include crossover bands such as Kíla or Osna. If you like unaccompanied Gaelic laments, ask to hear the heavenly voice of Finola Ó Siorchrú. If it's solo harp playing that you're looking for, check out the young artist from County Clare, Laoise Kelly, and her recent CD called *Just Harp*. Expect to pay IR£12-16/€15-20 for a CD.

### Dolphin Discs
**97 Talbot Street (C1)**
☎ 874 7438
**Open Mon.-Sat. 9.30am-6pm.**

A tiny shop with a fine selection of traditional music, including titles you can't get elsewhere, such as the superb album by Joe Boske entitled *Amara*. Of course, you'll also find the great classic groups (some of which are no longer together), such as Clannad and The Bothy Band, and the most popular ballad singers in Ireland, like the velvet-voiced Christy Moore and Mary Black and her younger sister Nancy. The only trouble is, you can't listen before buying. If you hear something you like in a pub, or elsewhere, don't be afraid to ask what it is – it's always a good way of starting a conversation.

### J. McNeill
**140 Capel Street (B2)**
☎ 872 2159
**Open Mon.-Sat. 10am-6pm.**

The craftsmen here make and repair all kinds of instruments used to play traditional and classical music. The shop front alone is a delight, with its display of fiddles, concertinas, harmonicas, banjos and *bodhráns*, or traditional drums. The shop has remained virtually

unchanged for over 150 years, and is the best place in the city to buy a traditional instrument. *Uileann pipes* range from IR£500-3,000/€635-3809 according to size.

## McCullough Pigott's

25 Suffolk Street (C2)
☎ 677 3138
Open Mon.-Sat. 9am-5.30pm.

If you fancy joining in the chorus on impromptu musical evenings in the pub, or you've always wanted to know all the words to 'Danny Boy', you'll find sheet music of all Ireland's traditional and most popular songs here (from IR£4/€5). The shop is one of the most highly respected in the city and also sells many different kinds of musical instruments, including *bodhráns* from IR£40/€51.

## COLLECTORS TAKE NOTE

Collectors hunting for old or rare books in English or Gaelic will find what they're looking for at **Cathach Books (C3)** (10 Duke Street, ☎ 671 8676, www.rarebooks.ie, Mon.-Sat. 9.30am-5.45pm). What's more, if you need a hand with tracking down an out-of-print title, they'll help you free of charge.

## Music Hall of Fame

57 Abbey Street Middle (C2)
☎ 878 3345
Open every day
10am-5.30pm.

Just inside the entrance of this interactive museum, you'll find a little shop with a very good stock of Irish music. Its great virtue lies in giving equal space to all the different types of music for which the Irish are famous, from folk

ballads and traditional to pop, rock and Afro-Celtic crossover. It's best to go there after visiting the museum, which will help you decide exactly what you want.

## Chapters

108-9 Abbey St Middle (C2)
☎ 872 3297
Open Mon.-Sat. 9.30am-6.30pm, Sun. noon-6.30pm.

This large bookshop is piled high with books, many on special offer, including fine volumes with photos of Ireland and Dublin itself. Take the time to browse round all the tables to discover original books on all kinds of interesting subjects, such as Celtic calligraphy, a dictionary of slang or the secrets of feng shui. It's worthwhile noting that the latest paperbacks often sell for less here than elsewhere (IR£5/€6 instead of IR£7/€9 or IR£8/€10). The second floor has a selection of CDs and videos.

## SOUVENIRS AND GIFTS

Like all big cities, Dublin has a
flourishing souvenir industry.
The main shops have several
outlets in various parts of the
capital. Predictably enough, most
of the articles on offer aren't made
in Ireland, but are imported cheaply
from the Far East. If you're prepared
to rummage around, you may come
up with something amusing and
inexpensive to take home.

### Colemans
**9 Westmoreland Street (C2)**
☎ **677 7531**
**Open every day 9am-9pm.**

One of the best-known names for
souvenirs, including postcards,
pencils and all kinds of knick-
knacks, as well as costume
jewellery, including brightly-
coloured brooches featuring
the ancient motifs seen in the
national museums for around
IR£10/€13. For Guinness
lovers, a reproduction of one
of the old advertisements
(IR£8-30/€10-38) will
make a perfect gift that will
look great in the kitchen.
There are also beautiful
posters of Dublin pub fronts
and Georgian doorways.

### Carrolls
**57 O'Connell Street
Upper (C1)**
☎ **873 5587**
**Open Mon.-Sat. 9.30am-
9pm, Sun. 10am-8pm.**

With vast displays of cheap
items on offer as presents or
souvenirs, Carrolls is the home
of Irish kitsch. Be prepared for
the worst – baseball caps in the
national colours, shamrocks
everywhere, and shirts, T-shirts
and glasses plastered with

Guinness and whiskey emblems.
Among all this there are a few
interesting items, such as sets of
beer mugs, Irish coffee-making
kits, fridge magnets, and CD
collections of drinking songs.

### The Source
### at Urbana
**43 Temple Bar (C2)**
☎ **670 3083.**

Ireland's wildest gift shop,
described by *Marie Claire* as
'the most exciting store in the
world'. The Source has original
gifts and toys with everything
geared for fun – miniature
slinkies (45p/€0.57), *Psycho*
shower curtains, naughty cupid
holograms, lava lamps, limited
edition retro Coca Cola fridge

(IR£1,750/€2,222), etc. A top seller is the ESX mini hot and cold portable fridge.

## Needlecraft

**27/28 Dawson Street (C3)**
☎ **677 2493**
**Email: needlecraft@iol.ie**
**Open Mon.-Fri. 9.30am-5pm.**

Knit your own Aran sweater or make a needlepoint heirloom for your family! Needlecraft is a splendid shop for any craft enthusiast. With a wide range of both economy and luxury yarns and patterns for knitting, needlepoint, embroidery and cross-stitch, it contains just about everything that demands needles and thread. The assistants are very knowledgeable and you'll be guided towards the level which best matches your expertise.

## Cinemania

**7 Eustace Street (B2)**
☎ **670 3665**
**Open Mon.-Thu. 10am-5.30pm, Fri. 10am-8pm, Sat. 10am-7pm, Sun. 1-7pm.**

If you want a miniature figurine of Keanu Reeves in the *Matrix*, or fancy a

tiny Austin Powers, this is the place to come. They stock all kinds of movie memorabilia including a selection of copies of original film posters. Fans of horror can indulge in the most gory and blood-thirsty toys and gadgets imaginable. For those of a more gentle persuasion, there's a good selection of Irish films on video.

## Evolution

**GPO Arcade (C2)**
**Henry Street**
☎ **872 0337**
**Open Mon.-Sat. 10am-6pm, Thu. 11.30am-7.30pm.**

## NATIONAL COLOURS

The Irish acquired their independence relatively recently, and have enormous pride in their national colours. Many Irish people left the island over the years in the successive crises, and there are a large number of expatriates all over the world who come back today as tourists. They are well catered for in the souvenir shops and markets with hats, belts, braces and T-shirts all in the national colours of green, white and orange.

You'll find bits and pieces from all four corners of the globe displayed in this shop. Little silk brocade make-up bags, lucky bracelets in every colour, dazzling pocket mirrors, Native American 'dream catchers' (from IR£5/€6), African wooden dishes and exotic masks make unusual, inexpensive presents. You're sure to find something to please everyone.

## GOURMET DELIGHTS

Ireland doesn't have much of a reputation as a gourmet paradise, but the time is long past when mutton, pork, cabbage and potatoes were the only Irish foods known. Among the local products, biscuits, sweets, teas and condiments are worth buying, and Dubliners are also enjoying the fact that the city has an increasing number of delicatessens and shops selling cheeses and speciality breads.

Johnson's Court. A charming little shop full of the aromatic smells of herbs and smoked produce, it has a great range of charcuterie, Irish cheeses and its own range of jams and chutneys (IR£2.50/€3.17), fresh Irish pâtés and wild Irish smoked salmon (IR£20-£35/ €25-44) which they will pack and deliver anywhere you want (IR£15/€19).

### Bewley's

**Grafton Street (C3)**
☎ 677 6761
**Open every day 7.30am-11pm.**

This Dublin institution, famous for its teas and coffees, also sells Guinness-flavoured toffees, strawberry and orange liqueur preserve, and some typically Irish cakes, including porter cake made with Guinness. Their teacakes, which should be lightly toasted before being served with butter and jam, are another teatime treat. The different blends of tea nicely packaged in wooden boxes make perfect gifts.

### Magill's Delicatessen

**14 Clarendon Street (C3)**
☎ 671 3830
**Open Mon.-Sat. 9.30 am-5.45pm.**

Ireland's oldest delicatessen, beloved by generations of Dubliners, is tucked away beside

### Epicurian Food Hall

**13-15 Liffey St Lower (C2)**
**Open every day 8.30am-7pm.**

This little shopping arcade is like a covered market, with a row

of shops to suit all tastes. The fishmonger sells excellent smoked salmon, and the Maison des Gourmets, a French pâtisserie, offers a selection of delicious cakes and pastries (IR£1.70-2.20/€2.15-2.80). There's also a bread shop, an Italian grocer, a wine merchant and a shop selling spices.

## Old Jameson Distillery

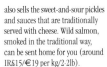

**Bow Street (A2)**
☎ 807 2355
**Open every day 9.30am-6pm.**

Even if you don't want to visit the distillery, there's a shop that sells sweets flavoured with Irish whiskey. If you want to take a bottle back, bear in mind that alcohol is pretty expensive in Ireland (IR£15/€19 for a bottle of Powers, IR£37/€47 for Jameson Reserve). You could simply settle for the whiskey-flavoured jams or cakes, the Irish coffee-flavoured fudge, or the whiskey-flavoured truffles or chutney (from IR£5)/€6.

## Sheridan's Cheesemongers

**11 Anne Street South (C3)**
☎ 679 3143
**Open Mon.-Sat. 9am-6pm.**

A little shop renowned for its Irish regional cheeses, Sheridan's

also sells the sweet-and-sour pickles and sauces that are traditionally served with cheese. Wild salmon, smoked in the traditional way, can be sent home for you (around IR£15/€19 per kg/2·2lb).

## Avoca

**11-13 Suffolk Street (C2)**
☎ 677 4215
**Open Mon.-Sat. 10am-6pm,
Thu. 10am-8pm**

A splendid food hall packed with enticingly delicious produce such as oils, preserves, jams, biscuits and chocolates all under the Avoca Pantry label (from £2/€2.50). Fresh food is prepared daily in the kitchen upstairs using only the best Irish ingredients to serve both the award-winning café on the 3rd floor and the food hall itself. Amongst other gourmet delicacies, choose from their famous 5 seed loaf (£2/€2.50), Mediterranean-style tarts, various hot dishes, such as leek, blue cheese and rocket fritatta and delectable pastries, while you relax over a coffee, or enjoy Sunday brunch as you listen to live jazz music in the café. *The Avoca Café Cookbook* (£17.99/€23) makes

### A MOUTHWATERING MARKET

Every Saturday morning, local producers set up their stalls for a small market held in Meeting House Square, in Temple Bar (C2). You can find traditional whiskey-flavoured fudge and fine hand-made chocolates here, as well as delicious tarts, cakes and biscuits, just like grandma used to make.

a lasting memento of this delicious refreshment stop and includes many of the recipes used in the café.

# BARGAIN CORNER

'Doing the sales' and bargain-hunting is almost a national sport in Ireland. There are discount stores, bargain shops and pound shops all over Dublin, as well as charity shops selling second-hand clothes. They're not much to look at from the outside, and many offer little of interest, but determined shoppers will find real bargains in some.

Irish golfing sweaters for men, in wool or cotton (£40-60/€50-76).

### The Harlequin
**13 Castle Market (C3)**
☎ 671 0202
**Open Mon.-Sat. 10am-6pm, (Sun. in summer only).**

A second-hand clothes shop with a good stock of leather jackets and coats, for men and women, in all colours of the rainbow. There are leather jackets in good condition from IR£20/€25, as well as a selection of barely worn tweed jackets that are far more affordable than new ones.

### Jenny Vander
**20 Market Arcade (off map)**
☎ 677 0406
**Open Mon.-Sat. 10am-6pm, Thu. 10am-7pm.**

Well known for her second-hand clothes, Jenny Vander stocks a wide choice of brightly coloured, extravagant items dating mainly from the 1950s and 60s. If you like the retro look, some of the evening dresses with bows and sequins are out of this world. You'll find pill-box and fur hats, modest lace blouses, stiletto shoes, little ladies' bags, and, above all, an amazing collection of enormous, sparkling

### The Sweater Shop
**9 Wicklow Street (C3)**
☎ 671 3270.

'Beautiful classics at reasonable prices', wrote *Vogue* of this excellent store. Traditional Aran sweaters are available both in original oiled wool (from IR£80/€102), and also soft and comfy merino wool (from IR£95/€120). You can get Irish designer knits from Mary Lavery, Foxglove Irish Linen Collection, and original one-off pieces by Gertrude Sampson (from IR£300/€380). Check out the super range of

## Half Price Jewellers

**27 Henry Street (C2)**
☎ 874 0368
www.hpj.co.uk
Open Mon.-Sat. 9am-
5.30pm, Sun noon-5pm.

All the jewellery here is claimed to be half price. The choice is limited to traditional 9 carat gold and silver pieces, which you choose from the window and order by filling in a slip supplied inside. You have to pay for your purchase before it's handed over at the counter, but you can have an immediate refund if you don't like it. Pretty gold chains cost from IR£25/€32 and Celtic crosses start at IR£15/€19.

costume jewellery. On the way out, have a quick look around the little arcade, which is a kind of flea market.

## Dunnes

**St Stephen's Green Shopping Centre**
☎ 478 0188
Open Mon.-Sat. 8.30am-7pm, Thu. 8.30am-9pm, Sun. noon-6pm.

There's terrific value in home ware at this popular chain store. As with their clothing range, Dunnes give an up-to-the-minute touch to all their own brand products. Competitive prices in excellent bed linen and soft furnishings, cookware, crockery and cutlery, lighting and bathroom wares. Look out for the stylish wood range which includes foldaway chairs (IR£14/€18), and really lovely beech picture frames (from IR£5/€6).

## The China Showrooms

**32/33 Abbey Street Lower**
☎ 878 6211

sales@chinashowrooms.ie
www.chinashowrooms.ie
Open Mon.-Sat. 10am-6pm.

This china shop has a lovely old fashioned feel. You can wander around the numerous table displays of well known brands of china and crystal glassware, both traditional and modern. With an excellent selection of giftware and collectables, you can always be sure of finding something on special offer – either a discontinued line or a stocktaking bargain. Great range of china mugs and figurines.

# Nightlife Practicalities

There are several ways to spend the evening in Dublin. The theatre is one of the major cultural attractions of the capital; despite being of high quality, dance performances, concerts of classical music and operas are less popular. In reality, the best evenings are the ones spent in the pub, an institution of Dublin life. After midnight, die-hards head for the clubs and late bars, where the young and trendy drink and dance until dawn.

## WHERE TO GO

If you want to live like a true Dubliner, the only place to spend your evenings is in the pub. It's a social institution, the place where people meet up to have a drink, to talk, and also to listen to the music that's such an integral part of Irish life. Most of the live gigs are supposed to start at around 9 or 9.30pm, but punctuality isn't an Irish virtue, so be prepared for a wait – possibly until as late as 10pm. You may be charged a small admission fee (IR£2-5/€2.50-6) in the evening, but you can often avoid it by arriving before 9pm. The bar stops serving at 11.30pm from Monday to Wednesday and Sunday, and 12.30am from Thursday to Saturday, but people tend to hang around for a bit longer.

The atmosphere in the nightclubs is totally different. People go there to see and be seen and to feel that they're part of the action. The clubs took off fairly recently as a result of the global success of Irish rock. In 1994, U2 opened their own club (see p. 124).

For the theatre-goer, Dublin is well provided with good venues. The Irish pride themselves on being a literary nation and the wealth of plays reflect their remarkable creativity. The classical concerts, ballets and operas, however, are less highly regarded, and only run for short seasons in the same theatres as the plays.

## THE LOOK THAT COUNTS

As in the UK, pubs are very informal with no particular dress code. They're open all day long, so people tend to come as they are to relax with a pint and enjoy the craic. There has, however, been a recent rise in the number of pubs employing doormen or 'bouncers'. These tend to be the more crowded places, frequented by young people, but some do have dress codes and the doorman may turn you away if you're wearing jeans or trainers.

Special dress codes do apply, however, in the clubs and late bars which are frequented by a very trendy clientele who could well be classed as fashion victims. Their priority is to make an impression. Girls wear ultra-short, low-cut dresses that show off the maximum of flesh, high-heeled sandals, and glittery accessories. To get into some clubs, you have to prove that you're interesting. If you don't feel like wearing anything too revealing, show a little imagination and assurance and try, in any case, to give the impression that the way you look is the right way.

## FINDING OUT WHAT'S ON

To find out what's on, whether it's concerts, plays, or pub and club events, buy the magazines *In Dublin* and *Hot Press* (IR£1.95/€2.50), which contain up-to-date information for the current fortnight. The free newspaper *The Event Guide* publishes the same details and is available from a number of places in the city (including the Irish Film Centre in Temple Bar and record shops).

Apart from some pubs, which are devoted entirely to traditional music or rock, most places, especially the nightclubs, don't play just one style of music, but change styles each evening, so it's best to find out beforehand what's on the programme. Hotels and some guest-houses have listings information, so don't hesitate to enquire at reception. Information can also be found on the website of the *Irish Times*, www.irishtimes.com; click on *Dublin Live*.

## BOOKING TICKETS

Ballet, opera and classical music rarely fill the theatres, and you should be able to get hold of tickets even if you do leave it until the last minute.

Some churches and halls stage free concerts during the daytime or early evening. However, rock and pop concerts, and performances by traditional music stars, sell out well in advance and you'll have little chance of finding a seat in the preceding fortnight. Seats for all performances can be booked on ☎ 456 9569 or through the tourist information office using your credit card (☎ 605 7777).

Depending on the type of performance, prices vary from IR£8-40/€10-50. On the evening of major concerts and

events, you could try to obtain tickets at the last moment from ticket touts in front of the concert venue, but they may be extremely expensive and quite often are not legitimate.

### ALCOHOL LICENSING LAWS

The sale of alcoholic beverages is strictly licensed in Ireland. They may only be sold in pubs until 11.30pm Mon.-Wed., 12.30am Thu.-Sat. (Sun. 12.30-11.30pm) and 2am in late bars. As the majority of clubs play music until gone 3am, they charge an admission fee (£4-8/€5-10) to cover their costs, and put up the price of drinks. Their clients still seem to drink copious amounts!

## THEATRES AND CONCERT VENUES

The same venues are used for different types of performances, including opera, which doesn't yet have a home of its own.

### Dublin Theatre Festival

For over 40 years, the annual Dublin Theatre Festival has been one of the most prestigious in Europe. Companies from all over the world come to perform in the city's theatres, foreign productions accounting for nearly half of the programme. For further information log on to the festival website www.eircomtheatre.com or ☎ 677 8439 (see also p. 20).

### The Abbey

**26 Abbey Street Lower (C2)**
**☎ 878 7222 (box office)**
**☎ 456 9569 (tickets)**
**Seats from IR£10-18.50/ €13-24.**

The Abbey has been home to the national theatre since 1904, and is an institution of Dublin cultural life. All the great plays in the Irish repertory were first staged here – and some were quickly censored! It's still one of the most creative theatres in the city, staging Irish classics, plays by young playwrights and public readings of works by new writers. Some plays by newer authors can be seen at lunchtime at a reduced price (under IR£5/€6.50).

### The Gate

**Parnell Square (C1)**
**☎ 874 4045**
**Seats at IR£15/€19 and IR£17/€22 (IR£12/€15 for previews).**

Dublin's other major theatre is smaller, and enjoys a more pleasant setting. Renowned for its eclecticism and daring, it staged plays by Oscar Wilde when they were prohibited in Britain. Orson Welles performed here at the start of his career. The programme features European and American plays

rather than the Irish classics, though Wilde still remains a favourite.

## Gaiety Theatre

**King Street South (C3)**
☎ **677 1717**
**Seats from IR£10-40/**
**€13-50.**

A cosmopolitan theatre that stages a variety of performances, ranging from classical productions and mainstream popular theatre, to opera and comedy. Some of most interesting and prestigious international productions are performed here and the tickets go up in price accordingly.

## Olympia

**72 Dame Street (B2-C2)**
☎ **677 7744**
**Seats from IR£8-25/€10-32.**

The Olympia serves up an eclectic programme during the first part of the evening, similar to that of the Gaiety – lots of variety shows, as well as ballet, jazz, and Irish and international stars. In the second part of the evening, at 11pm, the Midnight at the Olympia concerts turn the place into a kind of theatre café (with bars on all three

floors). Music ranges from jazz and blues to rock and rap. One of the best venues in the city.

## Andrew's Lane Studio & Theatre

**Andrew's Lane (off map)**
☎ **679 5720**
**Seats from IR£8-15/**
**€10-19.**

Plays and musical shows share the stage here, with high-class performances by Irish theatre companies. The productions are generally innovative and quite spectacular, with the accent on works by contemporary authors.

## National Concert Hall

**Earlsfort Terrace (C3)**
☎ **475 1572.**

Before becoming a concert hall, the building belonged to Dublin University, which probably explains its austere appearance and mediocre acoustics. Classical music is not well served in the Irish capital, so you shouldn't have any difficulty in getting last-minute tickets. The Friday lunchtime concerts make a pleasant break.

On the third Sunday in June, an exceptional music festival takes place here. From 1.30pm, a succession of free concerts is offered, with musical styles ranging from classical to jazz and rock. Some concerts are staged indoors, others in the courtyard and the nearby Iveagh Gardens.

## Bewley's Café

**Grafton Street (C3)**
☎ **677 6761**
**Seats at IR£7/€9 (soup and sandwich included).**

This small theatre on the second floor of the city's most famous café is a Dublin institution. Plays by Irish as well as international authors are performed here at lunchtimes (the doors open at 12.50pm). Don't miss it – it's very cosy and has all the atmosphere of a literary café.

## Hugh Lane Gallery

**Parnell Square North (C1)**
☎ **874 1903**
**Free concerts.**

From September to June, concerts of contemporary and chamber music are staged every Sunday afternoon in the elegant Georgian hall of the Municipal Art Gallery.

## The Point Depot

**Link Bridge East (off map)**
☎ **836 3633**
**Tickets IR£20-35/€25-44.**

Once a train depot, this vast hall on the north bank of the Liffey is 15 minutes' walk east of the centre, in the direction of the docks. It's now the setting for big rock and pop concerts but has also been the venue for *Riverdance*, a display by the Lippizaner stallions of the Spanish Riding School in Vienna, and *Disney on Ice*. Unfortunately, drinks and snacks are very expensive here, and the traffic is so bad at concert time that it's better to make your way here on foot.

## SFX Hall

**23 Sherrard Street Upper (off map)**
☎ **855 4673**
**Tickets IR£10-25/€12-32.**

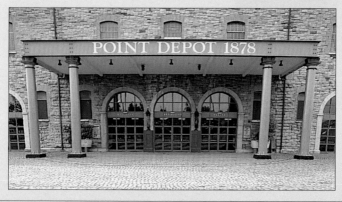

Although 'SFX' refers to St François Xavier, this hall is anything but church-like. U2 have made videos here, and hard rock and pop groups perform on its stage. However, it can't be reached by bus, and it's better not to come alone late at night. It's also a theatre venue.

## Temple Bar Music Centre

**Curved Street (off map)**
☎ 670 9202
**Tickets from IR£5/€6.**

A new hall close to the Irish Film Centre in the heart of Temple Bar that stages very different styles of concerts, including rock and traditional music, and even salsa. Dublin has recently gone salsa-crazy with dozens of classes being set up all over the city. One is held here on Tuesdays, 8-9pm, followed by a dance, so you can put what you've learnt into practice.

## Vicar Street

**99 Vicar Street
(Thomas Street-A3)**
☎ 454 6656 or 609 7788
**(Open 24hrs, reservations by credit card)
Tickets from IR£10-20/
€12.50-25.**

## Festivals

Around the weekend of 1 May, the Heineken Green Energy Festival brings together everything Ireland has to offer in the way of musicians and music for a massive festival of rock, blues, jazz and traditional music. Distinguished artists in the past have included The Cranberries, Kíla, and Tracy Chapman. Event follows event in venues all over the city. In July, the Temple Bar Blues Festival features fabulous open-air concerts on College Green (C2).

One of the in-places to listen to music and have a drink at the same time, with DJs and live groups on Friday and Saturday nights.

## HQ @ Hall of Fame

**57 Abbey Street Middle
(C2)**
☎ 889 94 99 (information)
☎ 456 9569 (tickets)
**Tickets IR£30-40/€38-50.**

Belonging to the interactive music museum, this venue stages live music concerts of every kind, from blues and jazz to rock and popular music.

## PUBS AND LATE BARS

All the traditional pubs have a sociable atmosphere in the evening. The selection that follows includes some that also offer music.

## O'Donoghue's

**15 Merrion Row (C3-D3)**
☎ 660 7194

One of the most famous traditional pubs in the city, and with good reason. The Dubliners, the band who brought traditional music back into fashion in the 1960s, made their debut here. Music is played every night from 9pm, but it's always packed, so be prepared to be jostled. Dubliners still come here, but there are more and more tourists. Plenty of enthusiasm, and a warm, friendly atmosphere.

## J.J. Smyth's

**12 Aungier Street (B3)**
☎ 475 2565.

This haunt of jazz and blues fans has been frequented by the same band of faithful for years. If you're interested in history, you may like to know that the pub occupies the house where the poet Thomas Moore was

born. The high-quality live music gigs featuring regular artists start at about 9.30pm, entry IR£4-5/€5-6.50.

## Eamon Doran's

**3A Crown Alley (C2)**
**☎ 679 9773.**

This is the place to come if you have an eclectic taste in music. On the first floor, after the restaurant has closed, there are concerts of traditional music on Friday and Saturday nights and Sunday afternoons. In an altogether different vein, the basement is one of the centres of Dublin rock, with concerts every evening from 9pm (IR£4-5/€5-6.50). More often than not, the music goes on until 2am. At weekends, there's music from midday onwards, with Saturdays open to new groups who want to try their luck.

## Whelan's

**25 Wexford Street (B3)**
**☎ 478 0766**
**Entry charge IR£5-8/€6.50-10.**

The concerts are very varied (Irish folk, world music, jazz and rock), and start at 8.30pm; allow time to queue for tickets. On some nights, Whelan's turns into a nightclub, with music playing until 2 or 3am. Check out the programme of the neighbouring establishment, The Mean Fiddler, which is also very lively in the evening.

## O'Shea's Merchant

**12 Bridge Street Lower (A2)**
**☎ 679 3797**
**Open every evening 9.30pm. Entry free.**

A unique, authentically Irish experience,

O'Shea's is the home of traditional Irish set dancing, in which couples or groups dance a number of set figures together. Provincial exiles in Dublin are particularly fond of the place, and guarantee it always has the light-hearted, easy-going atmosphere of a country club. Even novices will soon be drawn into the dance. Dinner is served before the performance.

## Harcourt Hotel

**60 Harcourt Street (C3)**
**☎ 478 3677**
**Entry free, nightclub IR£3-5/€3.80-6.50.**

Although known mainly for its traditional

A packed club, pleasantly decorated, with a good atmosphere and the distinct advantage of possessing its own concert hall at the back.

music, this hotel bar also hosts rock and pop evenings from time to time. Programme details are given in the local press and on the noticeboard. The interest of the place lies in the succession of musical genres. You can come here for traditional music from 9.30pm; if you then go on to the nightclub, you'll be in for a fairly conventional evening, with all the latest hits.

## Gaiety Theatre

**King Street South (C3)**
**☎ 677 1717**
**Entry charge IR£7.50-8.50/€9.50-10.50.**

This place is really a theatre (see p. 119), but on Friday and Saturday evenings, it turns into a nightclub from 11.30pm to 2.30am. Friday is Latin night, with a salsa band and a South American atmosphere. Saturday is soul and jazz night, which also goes with a swing.

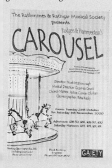

## The Norseman

**29 Essex Street East (B2)**
**☎ 671 5135**
**Entry free**

The Norseman is a favourite haunt of artists and musicians, however, it has also become very popular with tourists, who come here in droves to proclaim their Irish roots. The bar and

nightclub offers a cool, intimate atmosphere and traditional music concerts are staged on Friday and Saturday evenings which carry on late into the night.

## The George

**89 South Great Georges Street (B3)**
**☎ 478 2983**
**Entry IR£5-8/€6.50-10 (free before 10pm).**

A pub with a purple facade that's easy to spot, and which claims to be the heart of the capital's gay scene. The Block club upstairs even claims to be number one in Europe, with the best, the most vibrant and the liveliest nights. Although it's also open to lesbians and straight men and women, The George attracts a predominantly male clientele.

## The Quays

**12-13 Temple Bar (C2)**
**☎ 671 3922.**

The Quays opened relatively recently, but it looks as if it's been here forever. Lots of people come here in the evening, including a young, trendy clientele, for lively traditional music concerts on two floors.

## The Chocolate Bar

**Hatch Street Upper (off map)**
**☎ 478 0166.**

The trendiest bar in the city, with an incredible Gothic decor, and a mezzanine from which to survey operations. It's part of the PoD nightclub complex (see p. 124), but you can come here just for a drink. The cocktails are among the best in Dublin (IR£5/€6.50, half price during happy hour). Sunday is funk night. Arrive before 10pm to get into the PoD free.

### Free or fee?

Entry to the city's pubs is free, but on some nights, a charge is made for concerts, and from 9pm, you may be asked to pay IR£2-5/€2.50-6.50 according to the group who are playing and the pub. You can often avoid paying by arriving earlier and buying a drink, but try to find out exactly where the group will be performing. If it's upstairs or in another room, you'll still have to pay the entry fee.

## NIGHTCLUBS

### The Kitchen

**The Clarence Hotel
6-8 Wellington Quay
(B2-C2)
☎ 677 6635
Entry charge IR£7-8/
€9-10.**

This club may have been taken over by U2, but isn't as elitist as you might imagine, with a young clientele (20s-30s) unwinding to the sound of the latest dance music and techno sounds. The two underground vaulted rooms and dance floor surrounded by a moat make a rather unusual setting. The club isn't too difficult to get into, but they don't admit stag or hen parties.

doormen are very fussy about who they let in, so it's up to you to try to impress them with your appearance and convince them that your presence will only add to the scene inside. It's worth trying your luck just to get a glimpse of the fabulous decor.

### Rí Rá

**1 Exchequer Street (C2)
☎ 677 4835
IR£5-8/€6-10.**

A trendy basement club frequented by models and showbiz people. You might meet Irish stars, or at least people who

### Lillies Bordello

**Adam Court, Grafton Street
(C3)
☎ 679 9204
Entry charge IR£10/
€12.70.**

This is Dublin's ultimate trendy night spot, where fashion models come with their sugar daddies and film producers and other beautiful people come to be seen in the company of celebrities such as U2 and Boyzone. Of course, the

### PoD

**35 Harcourt Street (C3)
☎ 478 0166
Entry charge IR£4-8/€ 5-10.**

PoD stands for 'Place of Dance', another trendy club, with a glamorous decor and exotic clientele. It's known mainly for its HAM (Homo Action Movies) nights on Fridays, featuring trendy homo techno (straight men and women are also welcome). The music varies from techno to funk.

think they are. To get in, you'll need to be imaginative in your dress or just plain classy. If you want a quieter evening you can talk in peace in The Globe late bar on the ground floor. The DJs, on the whole, are excellent.

## The Ballroom @ Fitzsimon's

**Temple Bar (C2)**
☎ 677 9315.

This fairly traditional club housed in Fitzsimon's Hotel is famous for its theme nights and its selection of different DJs. In general they play a mix of old chart-toppers and more recent hits, with romance night on Sundays. At the start of the evening, also in the hotel, there are sessions of traditional music and dance that are very popular although touristy.

## The Sugar Club

**8 Leeson Street Lower (C3)**
☎ 678 7188.

The best cocktail bar in Dublin, The Sugar Club is a meeting place for the over-30s. An intimate, cosy setting, decorated in shades of red with cool, jazz, funk, groove and dance music. Try the somewhat surprising chocolate Martini (IR£4.50/€5.70).

## Renards

**35-37 Frederick Street South (C3)**
☎ 677 5876
**Café bar entry free, nightclub members only.**

Another place for the over-30s, spread over three floors, with a bar on each. It's fairly select, especially the VIP bar on the first floor. The nightclub in the basement (11pm-3am) is for members only. You can eat until 1am in the traditional bar on the ground floor.

## Red Box

**35 Harcourt Street (C3)**
☎ 478 0166
**Entry charge IR£5-10/ €6.50-12.50.**

Above PoD, and with very good music, guaranteed atmosphere, excellent acoustics and big international DJs.

## River Club

**Ha'penny Theatre
48 Wellington Quay (B2-C2)**
☎ 677 2382
**Entry charge IR£8/€10.**

Located in the Ha'penny Theatre, you can come here all day, from lunchtime until late at night, with its atmosphere that's cool and sophisticated. Frequented mainly by the over-30s, there's a strict dress code and a standard of elegance is required.

# Conversion tables for clothes shopping

## Women's sizes

### Shirts/dresses

| U.K | U.S.A | EUROPE |
|-----|-------|--------|
| 8 | 6 | 36 |
| 10 | 8 | 38 |
| 12 | 10 | 40 |
| 14 | 12 | 42 |
| 16 | 14 | 44 |
| 18 | 16 | 46 |

### Sweaters

| U.K | U.S.A | EUROPE |
|-----|-------|--------|
| 8 | 6 | 44 |
| 10 | 8 | 46 |
| 12 | 10 | 48 |
| 14 | 12 | 50 |
| 16 | 14 | 52 |

### Shoes

| U.K | U.S.A | EUROPE |
|-----|-------|--------|
| 3 | 5 | 36 |
| 4 | 6 | 37 |
| 5 | 7 | 38 |
| 6 | 8 | 39 |
| 7 | 9 | 40 |
| 8 | 10 | 41 |

## Men's sizes

### Shirts

| U.K | U.S.A | EUROPE |
|-----|-------|--------|
| 14 | 14 | 36 |
| $14^{1/2}$ | $14^{1/2}$ | 37 |
| 15 | 15 | 38 |
| $15^{1/2}$ | $15^{1/2}$ | 39 |
| 16 | 16 | 41 |
| $16^{1/2}$ | $16^{1/2}$ | 42 |
| 17 | 17 | 43 |
| $17^{1/2}$ | $17^{1/2}$ | 44 |
| 18 | 18 | 46 |

### Suits

| U.K | U.S.A | EUROPE |
|-----|-------|--------|
| 36 | 36 | 46 |
| 38 | 38 | 48 |
| 40 | 40 | 50 |
| 42 | 42 | 52 |
| 44 | 44 | 54 |
| 46 | 46 | 56 |

### Shoes

| U.K | U.S.A | EUROPE |
|-----|-------|--------|
| 6 | 8 | 39 |
| 7 | 9 | 40 |
| 8 | 10 | 41 |
| 9 | 10.5 | 42 |
| 10 | 11 | 43 |
| 11 | 12 | 44 |
| 12 | 13 | 45 |

### More useful conversions

| | | | |
|---|---|---|---|
| 1 centimetre | 0.39 inches | 1 inch | 2.54 centimetres |
| 1 metre | 1.09 yards | 1 yard | 0.91 metres |
| 1 kilometre | 0.62 miles | 1 mile | 1. 61 kilometres |
| 1 litre | 1.76 pints | 1 pint | 0.57 litres |
| 1 gram | 0.035 ounces | 1 ounce | 28.35 grams |
| 1 kilogram | 2.2 pounds | 1 pound | 0.45 kilograms |

This guide was written by **Christine Legrand**, with the collaboration of Véronique Basire, Sophie Janssens, Aurélie Joiris, Carine Merlin and Dominique Mével.
Translated by **Margaret Rocques**.
Copy editor **Jane Franklin**.
Series editor **Sofi Mogensen.**
Additional research and assistance Christine Bell, Helen Gallivan, Eivlin Roden, Kate Williams, Michael Summers.

The publisher would like to thank the Irish Tourist Board in Paris, and in particular Caroline Brunel and Anne Monks-Zemmour, for their valuable assistance.

We have done our best to ensure the accuracy of the information contained in this guide. However, addresses, phone numbers, opening times etc. inevitably change from time to time, so if you find a discrepancy please let us know. You can contact us at: hachetteuk@orionbooks.co.uk or write to us at Hachette UK, address below.

Hachette UK guides provide independent advice. The authors and compilers do not accept any remuneration for the inclusion of any addresses in these guides.

Please note that we cannot accept any responsibility for any loss, injury or inconvenience sustained by anyone as a result of any information or advice contained in this guide.

---

#### Photo acknowledgements

*Inside pages*
All the photographs in this book were taken by **Nicolas Edwige**, except for the following:

**Éric Guillot:** p. 19 (b.l.)
**Laurent Parrault:** p. 101 (c.)
**Photothèque Hachette:** p. 14 (c.), p. 15 (t.l.), p. 26 (c.l.), p. 26 (b.r.), p. 27 (t.l.), p. 34 (c.r.), p. 67 (c.r.), p. 88 (t.l.)
**Bord Fáilte – Irish Tourist Board:** p. 10 (c.l.), p.10 (c.r.), p. 11 (t.l.), p. 12 (c.l.), p. 13 (t.), p. 15 (c.), p. 20 (t.r.), p. 20 (c.l.), p. 29 (c.l.), p. 30 (b.l.), p. 31 (c.l.), Brian Lynch: p. 37 (c.l.)
**Bord Glas – Horticultural Development Board, Ireland:** p. 79 (b.r.)
**Arnotts:** p. 92 (l.), p. 98 (c.); **Avoca:** p. 98 (t.r.), p. 113 (b.r.); **Helen Cody:** p. 19 (t.l.); **Dunnes:** p. 115 (b.r.); **Michelle Garrett/CORBIS:** p. 111 (t.l.); **Susan Hunter:** p. 89 (b.r.); **Louise Kennedy:** p. 89 (b.l.), p. 93 (t.r.); **Kilkenny:** p. 87 (b.c.); **Magill's Delicatessen:** p. 112 (b.r.); **Thomas Patrick:** p. 91 (b.l.); **Quin & Donnelly (Brown Thomas):** p. 88 (t.r.); **John Rocha (Brown Thomas):** p. 107 (b.r.); **The Source:** p. 110 (b.r.); **Vivien Walsh:** p. 87 (t.r.).

*Front cover:*
All photographs by Nicolas Edwige except for:
**Stock Image, Pedro del Rio:** female figure, top band; **Hoa Qui, C. Casanova:** male figure, bottom band; **Superstock inc:** female figure centre right.

*Back cover:*
**Nicolas Edwige**

---

#### Illustrations
**Virginia Pulm**

First published in the United Kingdom in 2001 by Hachette UK

English Translation, revised and adapted, © Hachette UK 2001
Original French edition © Hachette Livre (Hachette Tourisme) 2001

Distributed in the United States of America by Sterling Publishing Co., Inc.
387 Park Avenue South, New York, NY 10016-8810

A CIP catalogue for this book is available from the British Library

ISBN 1 84202 096 X

Hachette UK, Cassell & Co., The Orion Publishing Group, Orion House, 5 Upper Saint Martin's Lane, London, WC2H 9EA

Printed and bound in Italy by Milanostampa

If you're staying on a little longer and would like to try some new places, the following pages will provide you with a wide choice of hotels, restaurants and bars, listed by district. Though you can just turn up at the door of a restaurant and have a meal (except in the most prestigious establishments), don't forget to book your hotel several days in advance (see p. 72).
Enjoy your stay!

# STAYING ON A LITTLE LONGER

# Hotels

## Around O'Connell Street

**Clifden House**
32 Gardiner Place
☎ 874 6364
**F** 874 6122
IR£50-110/€63-140.
*Unimaginative decoration, but a comfortable, well-kept hotel not far from O'Connell Street, with 14 rooms that are very reasonably priced in the low season.*

**Stella Maris**
13 Gardiner Street Upper
☎ 874 0835
IR£56/€71.
*Practically located only 5 minutes walk from O'Connell Street, and good value for money, with 8 unpretentious rooms and all mod cons. Credit cards not accepted.*

**Gardiner Lodge**
87 Gardiner Street Lower
☎ 836 5229
**F** 836 3279
IR£70/€90.
*A good, comfortable hotel within easy reach of the city centre that's cheap from 7 October to February. Payment made along with reservation.*

## Drumcondra Road

Buses 3, 11, 13A, 16, 16A, 33, 41.

**Willow House**
130 Drumcondra Road Upper
☎ 837 5733
IR£55/€70.
*All the rooms in this pleasant B&B are beautifully decorated in different styles. Equipped with hairdryers, kettles and TVs, they represent good value for money.*

**Applewood**
144 Drumcondra Road Upper
☎ 837 8328
IR£54/€68.50.
*Five very comfortable, if rather small, rooms. Each has a name that includes the word 'apple'. Pleasant and practical, like all the other accommodation in the street. The bus passes right by the door.*

**Arranmore**
104 Drumcondra Road Lower
☎ 830 0009
IR£45-50/€ 57-63.
*A tall Victorian house that's rather dark but very comfortable. In the low season, it's one of the least expensive places to stay in the city.*

**Errigal**
36 Drumcondra Road Upper
☎ 837 6615
IR£50/€63.
*Ten rooms with nondescript decoration that are a little noisy on the street side because of the nearby crossroads. The hotel is nevertheless very comfortable and can stand you in good stead if the other B&Bs are full.*

## Along the Liffey

**Eliza Lodge**
23-24 Wellington Quay
☎ 671 8044
**F** 671 8362
www.dublinlodge.com
IR£110/€140.
*A small, resolutely modern hotel with 18 light, practical rooms beside the river at the foot of the Millennium Bridge. Ideally located not far from Temple Bar, but a little expensive.*

**Arlington Hotel**
23-25 Batchelors Walk
☎ 804 9100
**F** 804 9112
www.arlington.ie
IR£110-140/€140-178.
*An unusual, medieval-style hotel with a very theatrical decor just next to O'Connell Bridge, with 116 well-equipped rooms, corridors dotted with armour and a bar with wall-to-wall panelling. The best prices are for two-night stays at the weekend, with special weekday offers in the low season.*

**Jury's Inn Custom House**
Custom House Quay
☎ 607 5000
**F** 829 0400
www.jurys.com
IR£71/€90.
*A big, impersonal hotel on the riverfront, 200m from Custom House in the direction of the docks, with 234 ultramodern rooms that are light and*
spacious. The rooms can hold 3 adults or 2 adults and 2 children. Breakfast isn't included in the price. More expensive on finals weekends.

## City centre

**Trinity Lodge**
12 Frederick Street South
☎ 679 5044
**F** 679 5223
IR£105-200/€133-250.
*This elegant Georgian building close to Trinity College has 13 rooms, all pleasantly decorated. They're rather small for the price, but perfectly comfortable, and Grafton Street is only 2 minutes away.*

**Adams Trinity Hotel**
28 Dame Street
☎ 670 7100
**F** 670 7101
IR£100-120/€127-152.
*A hotel in the heart of Temple Bar, with rather noisy rooms overlooking Dame Street. Ask for one at the back. The decor takes up the Irish medieval theme in a slightly artificial way. The dining room and bar arranged on several mezzanine floors are impressive. The price goes down if you stay for two successive nights.*

**River House**
23-24 Eustace Street
☎ 670 7655
**F** 670 7650
www.visunet.ie/riverhouse
IR£70-90/€89-114.
*A small hotel in the heart of Temple Bar that's comfortable but nondescript. Very practical if you want to walk home late at night. Otherwise a little expensive compared with places further from the centre.*

**Jury's Inn Christchurch**
Christchurch Place
☎ 454 0000
**F** 454 0012
www.jurys.com
IR£71/€90.
*A featureless building with 182 reasonably-priced rooms with all mod cons. Each room can hold 3 adults or 2 adults and 2 children. Breakfast is extra. Very centrally located opposite Christchurch, less than 5 minutes from Temple Bar.*

## Academy Hotel
Findlater Place
☎ 878 0666
🖷 878 0600
www.academy-hotel.ie
IR£80-160/€102-203.
*This comfortable modern hotel is very well located at the top of O'Connell Street. Ask for rooms that face east, as the neighbouring bar on the west side is noisy in the evening.*

## Temple Bar Hotel
Fleet Street
☎ 677 3333
🖷 677 3088
IR£90-140/€114-178.
*In the hustle and bustle of Temple Bar, an international-style hotel with 129 very comfortable rooms offering special weekend breaks (Friday and Saturday nights).*

### St Stephen's Green and Merrion Square

## Shelbourne
27 St Stephen's Green
☎ 676 6471
🖷 661 6006
www.shelbourne.ie
IR£195-500/€248-635 plus.
*A legendary hotel where the old-fashioned luxury conjures up the years of English rule. Ever popular, it offers high-class decor, discreet elegance, and a view of the park.*

## Longfield's
Fitzwilliam Street Lower
☎ 676 1367
🖷 676 1542
IR£135-170/€171-216.
*A charming, luxurious little hotel south of Merrion Square, 5 minutes from St Stephen's Green. In keeping with its Georgian style, it offers fine antique furniture, fireplaces, moulded ceilings and first-class service. The rooms with four-poster beds are the most expensive.*

## Staunton on the Green
83 St Stephen's Green
☎ 478 2300
🖷 478 2263
IR£110-120/€140-152.
*A large Georgian house on the south side of the Green with vast, light rooms. The decor may be a little old-fashioned, but you get a warm welcome and an excellent location less than 5 minutes' walk from Grafton Street.*

## The Fitzwilliam
41 Fitzwilliam Street Upper
☎ 662 5155
🖷 676 7488
www.fitzguests.ie
IR£80-95/€102-121.
*A few minutes from Grafton Street, 13 pleasantly decorated rooms, a warm welcome and efficient service. November to April is the cheapest time of year.*

### Ballsbridge

Buses 5, 6, 7, 8 and 45.

## Ariel House
Lansdowne Road
☎ 668 5512
🖷 668 5845
IR£87-186/€110-236.
*This fine Victorian mansion will give you a taste of 19th-century high-society life. The 40 elegant rooms, some of which are in a modern annexe, are all of different sizes. With a fairly complex pricing system in operation, the rate depends on the type of room, and is negotiable in the low season.*

## Merrion Hall
54 Merrion Road
☎ 283 8155
🖷 283 7877
www.greenbook.ie/merrion
IR£95-135/€121-171.
*A small, discreet hotel with 23 conservatively smart rooms. Very comfortable, though the welcome is rather formal.*

## Bewley's
Merrion Road
Ballsbridge
☎ 668 1111
🖷 668 1999
www.bewleyshotels.com
IR£69/€88.
*An amazing red-brick complex built round an old boarding school. A rather impersonal hotel with 220 rooms, restaurants and bars. The rooms are big enough for 3 adults and there's a bus stop right outside the door. Breakfast extra.*

**66 Townhouse**
66 Northumberland Road
☎ 660 0333
🅕 660 1051
Buses 5, 7, 7A, 8, 45, 46
and 84
IR£75-120/€95-152.
*Nine light, spotless rooms
on a fine, shady avenue.
Very comfortable despite its
lack of character.*

**Redwood Lodge**
78 Merrion Road
☎ 668 5019
🅕 668 7336
IR£70-80/€89-102.
*An imposing Victorian house
offering 16 spacious rooms that
are light and very well equipped,
with a bus stop in front of the
door. Noisy in the daytime
because of a crossroads, but
quiet at night.*

# HOTELS

# Restaurants

## Around O'Connell Street

### Writers Museum Café
18 Parnell Square
☎ 873 2266
Open every day
10am-4.30pm.
*The museum cafeteria is an annexe of the excellent Chapter One restaurant next door. It serves salads, quiches and exotic dishes for under IRE6/€7.50, and is the ideal place for lunch. You can also have tea, cakes and scones. On fine days, the Zen garden is delightful.*

### Madigan's
19 O'Connell Street.
☎ 874 0646.
*One pub among many, but this one serves generous helpings of good, simple dishes for lunch. You can eat here for IRE4-6/ €5-7.50 and enjoy the beer at the same time.*

### Clery's Café
O'Connell Street
☎ 878 6000
Open Mon., Tue., Sat.
9am-6.30pm, Thu. 9am-9pm, Fri. 9am-8pm.
*A useful place for a lunch or tea break while out shopping. This little cafeteria on the first floor of Clery's department store offers sandwiches, snacks and pastries for under IRE5/€6.50 in an old-fashioned English-style setting.*

## Near the Liffey

### The Winding Stairs Café
40 Ormond Quay Lower
☎ 873 3292
Open Mon., Tue,. Wed.,
Sat. 9.30am-6pm, Thu.-Fri. 9.30am-8pm, Sun. 1-6pm.
*This small restaurant perched above the Liffey is at the top of a spiral staircase lined with books and posters. The clientele is friendly and varied, and there's a lovely view of the Ha'penny Bridge. Ideal for lunch or tea.*

### Pravda
38 Liffey Street Lower
☎ 874 0076
Open Mon.-Fri. noon-12.30am, Sat.-Sun.
noon-2.30am.
*A young, trendy place, with brick walls, wooden floors, Soviet-style frescoes and candlelit booths. On the menu are stuffed 'wraps' and spicy chicken wings for under IRE5/€6.50.*

### Kielys Fusion Food
Abbey Street Upper
☎ 872 2100
Open Mon.-Wed.
10.30am-11.30pm,
Thu. 10.30am-12.30am,
Fri., Sat. 10.30am-1am,
Sun. 12.30pm-11.30pm.
*One entrance takes you into an old-fashioned pub, the other into an ultra-modern restaurant serving very varied cuisine, from smoked salmon on fresh baguette to fillet of duck breast salad or grilled lamb chops. Around IRE5/€6.50 for a snack, and IRE9-13/€11-17 for main courses.*

## Near Trinity College

### Kilkenny Café
6 Nassau Street
☎ 677 7066
Open Mon.-Sat. 9am-6pm, Thu. 9am-8pm, Sun. 11am-6pm.
*A quiet restaurant offering a variety of sandwiches and mixed salads, as well as more elaborated dishes and cakes, in one of the finest craft shops in the city. You can have a hearty meal for well under IRE10/ €12.70 here.*

### Tosca
20 Suffolk Street
☎ 679 6744
Open every day. 12.30-5.30pm, 6.30-11pm.
*A modern decor with temporary exhibitions on the walls is the setting for classic Italian cuisine. From IRE6/€7.50 for lunch, and IRE12-15/€15-19 for dinner.*

## Around Grafton Street

### The Duke
9 Duke Street
☎ 679 9553.
*A friendly pub where you can have lunch in a cosy setting for IRE5-8/€6.50-10. Straight-forward dishes and good plain home cooking in a place that's made literary history.*

### La Mère Zou
22 St Stephen's Green
☎ 661 6669
Open every day 12.30-2.30pm, 6-10.30pm, closed Sat. and Sun. lunchtimes.
*Good Franco-Belgian cuisine, with mussel and lamb specialities. The 'Big Plates' are generous helpings of themed food for IRE9.50/€12. Set lunch IRE12.50/€16, dinner IRE22.50/€28.50. Early bird 6-7.30pm IRE14.50/€18.50 (exc. Sat.).*

### Dome Restaurant
St Stephen's Green Centre
☎ 478 1287
Open Mon.-Sat. 9am-5.30pm.
*Airy self-service restaurant with great views over St Stephen's Green. Selection of hot foods, salads, pizzas and vegetarian dishes . Expect to pay around IRE5-8/€6.50-10. Live guitar music every afternoon.*

### Café Kylemore
St Stephen's Green Shopping Centre, 1st floor
☎ 478 1657
Open Mon.-Wed., Sat. 9am-6pm, Thu.-Fri. 9am-8pm, closed Sun.
*This cafeteria with a view of St Stephen's Green allows you to watch the world go by while eating simple cuisine at a wide range of prices. A practical place to stop for lunch or tea while out shopping.*

### Kaffe Mocha
39 William Street South
☎ 671 0978
Open Mon.-Fri. 9am-12.30am, Sat.-Sun. 9am-midnight.
*A trendy place ideal for late-night snacks at the weekend. Fairly loud rock music, hot and cold sandwiches from IRE5/ €6.30 and pizza or pasta for around IRE7.50/€9.50.*

### Cornucopia
19 Wicklow Street
☎ 677 7583
Open Mon.-Sat. 9am-8pm, Thu. 9am-9pm.
*A very popular vegetarian restaurant serving light, healthy dishes that make a welcome change from pub food. Try the salads or vegetable quiches. A meal costs around IR£6/€7.50.*

## Temple Bar

### Oliver St John Gogarty
58-59 Fleet Street
☎ 671 1822.
*This is the place to come for Sunday lunch (12.30-2pm) while listening to traditional live music. It gets packed, but the atmosphere is fantastic, and everyone joins in with the choruses. You can have a very generous helping of traditional Irish stew for under IR£7.50/ €9.50. For dinner, the restaurant on the first floor is more formal and more expensive.*

### Elephant & Castle
18 Temple Bar
☎ 679 3121
Open Mon.-Fri. 8am-11.30pm, Sat. 10.30am-11.30pm, Sun. noon-11.30pm.
*This restaurant serving high-quality American cuisine in generous helpings is always packed, though the burgers and chips and grilled meats are rather expensive.*

### Gallagher's Boxty House
20-21 Temple Bar
☎ 677 2762
Open Mon.-Sat. noon-11.30pm.
*A Temple Bar institution, now very popular with tourists, specializing in boxties - potato pancakes with various fillings (around IR£8-10/ €10-13).*

## Dublin Castle and Francis Street

### Frères Jacques
74 Dame Street
☎ 679 4555
Open Mon.-Fri. 12.30-2.30pm, Sat.-Sun. 7.30-10.30pm.
*French country cooking, including rustic soups, leg of lamb in a crust, snails with garlic, and traditional desserts. The bill soon exceeds IR£15/€19.*

### Shalimar
17 South Great Georges Street
☎ 671 0738
Open Mon.-Thu. 12.30-2.30pm, 6pm-midnight, Fri.-Sat. 12.30pm-midnight, Sun. 1pm-1am.
*A wide variety of Indian dishes and an early-bird set meal until 7pm (starter, main course and tea or coffee). Meals are served in a large, candlelit room with an Indian decor. If you don't like your food too hot, check the spiciness on the menu.*

### Juice
73 South Great Georges Street
☎ 475 7856
Open Mon.-Wed. 9am-11pm, Thu.-Fri. 9-4am, Sat. noon-4am, Sun. noon-11pm.
*Healthy, mainly vegetarian, organic food, and long glasses of delicious fruit or vegetable juice - ideal for the morning after too much Guinness or whiskey. Lunch for under IR£6/€7.50, dinner IR£10-12/€12.50-15.*

### O'Donohoe's
2 Lord Edward Street
☎ 677 0627
Open Mon.-Sat. 9am-6pm, Sun. 10am-6pm.
*A good place to eat very cheaply next to Christchurch, serving salads, sandwiches, lasagne and Irish stew for IR£2-5.50/ €2.50-7.*

## South of Stephen's Green

### Number Ten
Fitzwilliam Street Lower
☎ 676 1367
Open Mon.-Fri. 12.30-2.30pm, 6.30-10pm, Sat.-Sun. 6.30-10pm.
*A mixture of flavours from a variety of places for inventive cuisine that's sometimes a bit too elaborate. The simplest dishes are the best. Expect to pay over IR£14/€18 at lunchtime and over IR£29/€37 in the evening.*

**RESTAURANTS**

# Excursions in the Dublin area

*If you decide to stay on a few days longer in Dublin, here are three very pleasant excursions that will give you an idea of the country's charm. They're easy to do in a day, leaving the centre of Dublin by bus. If you prefer to hire a car, the sites are all within a 60 km/38 mile radius of the city. The first takes you on a voyage of discovery of the people of the Neolithic Age.The second takes you to the heart of a 6th-century monastery that was once one of the largest in the island. The last gives an insight into the privileged lifestyle of the Anglo-Irish aristocracy, with their great houses set in beautiful gardens.*

## NEWGRANGE AND THE BOYNE VALLEY

If you want to get here by bus, a special service leaves the Busaras (Central Bus Station) in Store Street (and from several other stops) every day except Friday (not in Jan.) at 10am (returning at 4.15pm or 5.45pm (according to season), IRE16/€20 in low season, and IRE20/€25 in high season (☎ 836 6111). *Mary Gibbons Tours* (☎ 283 9973) runs the same excursion from various points in the city, such as the tourist information office (leaving at 1.20pm, and returning at around 6.30pm, IRE16/€20). In both cases, entry to the site is included in the price. The trip to Newgrange includes a detour by way of Tara or Mellifont and Monasterboice, alternately, according to the day of the week. If you're driving take the N2 direct to Newgrange, then carry on north along it until you come to Mellifont, and later Monasterboice. If you prefer to go via Tara, take the N3 to Navan, to the north-west of Dublin.

In a pastoral landscape to the north of Dublin, the Boyne Valley is home to a number of highlights of Irish heritage. The oldest and most famous is Newgrange, a Neolithic passage-tomb mound of impressive dimensions. It's over 5,000 years old, and one of the finest in the world. The artistic sense of those who built it is revealed in the fine engraved stones, and the tomb layout also shows their knowledge of astronomy. The tomb is built in such a way that the sun lights up the funeral chamber on the winter solstice, symbolizing both the passage to the other world and the arrival of the new year, and the start of the natural cycle. The peaceful valley also houses the remains of two important abbeys, Mellifont and Monasterboice. Mellifont, the first Cistercian abbey in Ireland, founded in 1142, has retained its elegant cloister. Monasterboice, which is far older, is known above all for its three magnificent 10th-century Celtic crosses sculpted with scenes from the Bible, and for its 9th-century round tower. Further west, the royal hill of Tara, seat of the ancient Celtic kings and the subject of legends, is dotted with Iron Age tombs and forts. The valley was also the scene of the fateful Battle of the Boyne in 1690, in which William of Orange defeated James II of England.

## GLENDALOUGH AND THE WICKLOW MOUNTAINS

*Several organized excursions take in the magical site of Glendalough from Dublin, run by Bus Éireann (leaving Busaras in Store Street at 10.30am, and returning at 4.30 or 5.45pm, according to season), Mary Gibbons Tours (leaving the tourist information office at 12.45pm, and returning at 5 or 6.45pm according to season), and Over The Top Tours (leaving the tourist information office at 9.45am, and returning at 5.30pm). Tickets cost IRE15-20/€19-25 for the return trip.*

By car, take the N11 south in the direction of Wexford, fork off towards Enniskerry, then carry on west to Glencree. You then turn south to cross Sally Gap and reach Glendalough, about 50km/30 miles from Dublin.

The Wicklow Mountains rising south of the capital offer one of the finest landscapes in the region. The road runs through empty, desolate hills, crossed by raging torrents, and inhabited by black-headed sheep. A traditional feature of Ireland, piles of black peat lie on the surface among the heather and rough grass. Founded by St Kevin in the 6th century, Glendalough is one of the oldest monasteries in the country. The delightful greystone group includes the chapel, the cathedral, the oratories, the monks' cells and round towers, all set in a landscape of wooded mountains. The walk along the banks of the nearby pool is very enjoyable.

## POWERSCOURT DEMESNE

*Lying 23km/14 miles south of Dublin, via the N11 and Enniskerry, Powerscourt Demesne is also accessible by bus from the city centre. Mary Gibbons Tours combines this excursion with a visit to Glendalough (leaving at 12.45pm from the tourist information office, returning at 5 or 6.45pm; price IRE17/€22). Bus Éireann contents itself with taking customers as far as Sally Gap to see the Wicklow Mountains after visiting Powerscourt Gardens (leaving from Busaras in Store Street at 10am, returning at 5pm, IRE20/€25 (Tuesdays only Jun.-Sep.).*

The imposing Palladian mansion is a typical example of the grand houses built by British landlords. The fabulous terraced gardens offer a marvellous view over the little lake and beyond, to the Wicklow Mountains.

# EXCURSIONS

**NOTES**

**NOTES**

**NOTES**

# HACHETTE TRAVEL GUIDES

*Titles available in this series:*
A GREAT WEEKEND IN AMSTERDAM  (ISBN: 1 84202 002 1)
A GREAT WEEKEND IN BARCELONA  (ISBN: 1 84202 005 6)
A GREAT WEEKEND IN BERLIN  (ISBN: 1 84202 061 7)
A GREAT WEEKEND IN BRUSSELS  (ISBN: 1 84202 017 X)
A GREAT WEEKEND IN FLORENCE  (ISBN: 1 84202 010 2)
A GREAT WEEKEND IN LISBON  (ISBN: 1 84202 011 0)
A GREAT WEEKEND IN LONDON  (ISBN: 1 84202 013 7)
A GREAT WEEKEND IN MADRID  (ISBN: 1 84202 095 1)
A GREAT WEEKEND IN NAPLES  (ISBN: 1 84202 016 1)
A GREAT WEEKEND IN NEW YORK  (ISBN: 1 84202 004 8)
A GREAT WEEKEND IN PARIS  (ISBN: 1 84202 001 3)
A GREAT WEEKEND IN PRAGUE  (ISBN: 1 84202 000 5)
A GREAT WEEKEND IN ROME  (ISBN: 1 84202 169 9)
A GREAT WEEKEND IN VENICE  (ISBN: 1 84202 018 8)
A GREAT WEEKEND IN VIENNA  (ISBN: 1 84202 026 9)

*Coming soon:*
A GREAT WEEKEND IN BUDAPEST  (ISBN 1 84202 160 5)

## HACHETTE VACANCES

Who better to write about France than the French?
A series of colourful, information-packed, leisure and activity guides for
family holidays by French authors. Literally hundreds of suggestions for
things to do and sights to see per title.

*Titles available:*
BRITTANY  (ISBN: 1 84202 007 2)
CATALONIA  (ISBN: 1 84202 099 4)
CORSICA  (ISBN: 1 84202 100 1)
DORDOGNE & PÉRIGORD  (ISBN: 1 84202 098 6)
LANGUEDOC-ROUSSILLON  (ISBN: 1 84202 008 0)
NORMANDY  (ISBN: 1 84202 097 8)
POITOU-CHARENTES  (ISBN: 1 84202 009 9)
PROVENCE & THE COTE D'AZUR  (ISBN: 1 84202 006 4)
PYRENEES & GASCONY  (ISBN: 1 84202 015 3)
SOUTH-WEST FRANCE  (ISBN: 1 84202 014 5)

## ROUTARD

Comprehensive and reliable guides offering insider advice for the
independent traveller.

*Titles available:*
CALIFORNIA, NEVADA & ARIZONA  (ISBN: 1 84202 025 0)
IRELAND  (ISBN: 1 84202 024 2)
PARIS  (ISBN: 1 84202 027 7)
THAILAND  (ISBN: 1 84202 029 3)

*Coming soon:*
ANDALUCIA & SOUTHERN SPAIN  (ISBN 1 84202 028 5)
BELGIUM  (ISBN: 1 84202 022 6)
CANADA  (ISBN: 1 84202 031 5)
CUBA  (ISBN: 1 84202 062 5)
GREEK ISLANDS & ATHENS  (ISBN: 1 84202 023 4)
NORTHERN BRITTANY  (ISBN: 1 84202 020 X)
PROVENCE & THE COTE D'AZUR  (ISBN: 1 84202 019 6)
ROME & SOUTHERN ITALY  (ISBN: 1 84202 021 8)